A GRACEFUL LIFE

A GRACEFUL LIFE

Lutheran Spirituality for Today

Bradley Hanson

Augsburg

MINNEAPOLIS

A GRACEFUL LIFE
Lutheran Spirituality for Today

Cover design by Dave Meyer
Book design by Timothy W. Larson

Library of Congress Cataloging-in-Publication Data
Hanson, Bradley.
  A graceful life: Lutheran spirituality for today / Bradley Hanson.
    p. cm.
  Includes bibliographical references.
  ISBN 0-8066-3806-0 (alk. paper)
  1. Spiritual life—Lutheran Church. 2. Lutheran Church—Doctrines. I. Title.

BV4501.2.H336 1999
248.4'841—dc21   99-53604

Manufactured in the U.S.A.   AF 9-3806

04   03   02   01   00   1   2   3   4   5   6   7   8   9   10

For Sophie, whose smile brightens the day

CONTENTS

PREFACE

A BOOK ON LUTHERAN SPIRITUALITY is likely to meet a variety of responses. I hope the majority will say, "Good, I've been waiting for this." But there will be others, some Lutherans among them, who will ask, "Lutheran spirituality—isn't that an oxymoron, a contradiction in terms?" Much depends on one's understanding of the term *spirituality*. Since there is no universally accepted meaning of the word, readers will come with differing preconceptions and expectations. Obviously, the book cannot satisfy all those expectations. Nonetheless, my hope is that it will be a step forward in understanding Lutheran spirituality. The primary intended audience for this book is the average person, Lutheran or non-Lutheran, who might look to the Lutheran tradition for instruction and spiritual nurture. At the end of each chapter are some exercises for reflection and practice that are suitable for use either by a single reader or a group. These exercises are an integral part of the whole, for spirituality is not just a set of ideas, but rather a lived reality.

A brief comment about my approach. Bernard McGinn distinguishes three different approaches to the study of spirituality: anthropological, historical, and theological.[1] The anthropological approach views spirituality chiefly as a human quest for meaning that finds expression in a host of outlooks both religious and secular. The historical procedure carefully traces the development of a spirituality through time. The theological method concentrates on the theological outlook that gives shape to a particular spirituality. Perhaps it is not surprising, since I am a systematic theologian, that my predominant method is theological.

Yet there is more than personal penchant to justify a theological approach to Lutheran spirituality, for the Lutheran faith is so thoroughly informed by a coherent theological vision. This focus means, though, that the book pays considerably less attention to the concerns of those oriented more to an anthropological or historical method. In respect to the anthropological concern, I think I'm faithful to the Lutheran tradition in recognizing both a divinely given, restless longing for God in human beings and our utter dependence on divine grace for truly satisfying this longing. In regard to the historical approach, there are many questions about whether and how Lutherans used a particular prayer practice, musical form, or preaching style, but for the most part I don't think such issues are determinative of what makes a spirituality Lutheran.[2] What counts most is the theological vision that informs the spirituality.

The text of this book was almost in final form when I received a copy of "Spirituality and Spiritual Formation," a position paper adopted in October 1998 by the faculty of Lutheran Theological Southern Seminary. I'm happy to say that I agree almost entirely with what is stated there; my differences are mostly in emphasis or certain uses of terminology. My conversation with that document will occur largely in the notes.

I am grateful to a number of people who have helped me in writing this book. At the beginning, Ron Klug, an editor at Augsburg Fortress Publishers, was instrumental in getting the project off the ground. When I first sent a proposal for a very different kind of book on Lutheran spirituality several years ago, Ron said that particular project was not viable, but he invited me to talk further with him about a volume on this topic. Several old and new friends helped give me some exposure to Lutheranism outside the United States—in Germany, Superintendent Dieter Henkelmann and Lore Henkelmann, and in Tanzania, Shoonie Hartwig and the faculty of Lutheran Theological College at Makumira. Close to the end of the undertaking, my friend Ralph Quere, professor of church history at Wartburg Theological Seminary and an expert in the Reformation and Lutheran confessions, carefully reviewed a penultimate version and made numerous helpful suggestions. I am very thankful to him for that time-consuming aid. Whatever inadequacies that remain are my own responsibility. Throughout the writing process, I have benefited from the wise counsel of Marion Hanson, my wife, and from the input and responses of numerous people with whom I have shared some of these ideas. And Judy Boese of Luther College deserves high praise for her cheerful and expert help at all stages of manuscript preparation.

1

CONTEXT
PRESENT AND PAST

ALL OF US ARE ON A SPIRITUAL JOURNEY. We are beings with
spirits. The basic meaning of *spirit* is to transcend, to stand
beyond oneself. As spiritual beings, we are able to transcend our
immediate circumstances and ask whether there is a greater reality
and a larger meaning to which we may appropriately give ourselves.
Our spiritual journeys are driven in good part by our search for an
answer to this question. All of us end up answering the question by
the actual course of our lives, for our daily choices reflect what is the
greatest reality for us.

God is also on a journey that launches, sustains, and seeks to guide
our own. God is engaged in the stupendous project of creating this vast
universe and bringing it to fulfillment. God made us spiritual beings
who look for a greater reality to which we may give our highest trust and
loyalty. God is also Spirit who is present within the world, striving to
guide us in our journeys. Long ago, Augustine, in the opening paragraph
of his *Confessions,* said to God, "Thou has formed us for Thyself, and our
hearts are restless till they find rest in Thee."[1] I believe this is an accurate
reading of the human situation. God has created us as spiritual beings
whose lives are meant to be centered on God. As the source of everything else, God is the only reality to which we may appropriately give our
highest trust and loyalty. So within us there is a longing for God.

Although God is intended to be central, we tend to give other
things that position. It may be our families, ourselves, money, alcohol,
any number of things. Whatever we put in God's place, though, will
not finally satisfy. As Augustine wrote, "Our hearts are restless until

they find rest in Thee." Our spiritual journeys are, therefore, motivated both by a deep desire to find a higher meaning and by a longing to be healed, to be made whole, to find true rest.

God is not far off, but near. Nearer than we usually recognize. Our spiritual journeys have not only been launched by the one who created us, but they are undergirded by the divine Spirit who seeks to bring us and all other creatures to fulfillment. In each instant, God is seeking dialogue with us. In the rising and setting sun, in the encouragement of a friend, in the complaints of a family member, in the responsibilities of our daily work, and in countless other ways, God speaks to us. Of course, most of the time we are deaf to God's voice. The sweet truth in all this, though, is that God is not in hiding. Our search for God is grounded in God's search for us and in God's desire to communicate with us. Our restless hearts will find rest the more deeply we enter into dialogue with God.

life

THE CULTURAL CONTEXT

Although the particular events and circumstances of our lives put each of us on a unique spiritual journey, the way in which we go about our spiritual journey is influenced by the culture and society in which we live. This cultural context forms the broad terrain through which we must travel. It is prudent to survey this terrain and become aware of its broad contours. In contemporary American culture, three factors powerfully affect the ways many Americans live out their spirituality: increased social pluralism, greater individual autonomy, and and more elective ties to religious institutions. These three factors are strong throughout Western culture and, in varying degrees, are manifest in many other cultures. We shall examine each factor in turn.

1. *Increased social pluralism.* Compared to most European countries, the United States has always been more socially and religiously diverse. Whereas most states in Europe had an established church that only gradually granted tolerance to others, from the beginning the United States brought together many different religious believers. Over time, that degree of pluralism has greatly expanded. Not only has the United States given birth to new forms of Christianity such as

the Church of Jesus Christ of Latter-day Saints and Jehovah's Witnesses, but it has been fertile ground for other religious and quasi-religious movements such as spiritualism and Theosophy in the nineteenth century and Scientology in the twentieth century. In addition to substantial groups that follow a purely secular faith, there are rapidly growing numbers of adherents to every major religious tradition in the world now living in the United States. Other Western nations are experiencing a similar expansion of religious and spiritual diversity. A visit to any large bookstore in a Western country reveals a wide array of volumes on all the major world religions as well as books under headings like spirituality, New Age, occult, and Wicca. Westernized nations have become spiritual and religious supermarkets with a tremendous variety of offerings.

2. *Greater individual autonomy.* Individualism has always been a strong element within American culture, but in recent decades the sense of personal choice has increased substantially. Of course, individuality is part of our makeup as humans, just as is belonging to a community such as the family. In fact, individuality and community are like the negative and positive poles of a magnet; one cannot exist without the other. Nevertheless, cultures differ in the relative weight they give to individuality or community. In traditional African cultures, generally the primary weight falls on community. This is evident in religious life; for instance, when a Masai leader turns from his traditional religion to Christianity, many others in the community also become Christian. This attitude is also behind New Testament accounts about missionary activity in the Greek city of Philippi where Lydia "and her household" and the jailer "and his entire family" were baptized (Acts 16:15, 33). In the United States and most Western nations, however, the primary weight has been placed on the individual. In response to the Gallup poll question, "Do you think a person can be a good Christian or Jew if he or she doesn't attend church or synagogue?" 76 percent of Americans answered yes.[2] An even higher 81 percent agreed that one should arrive at his or her own religious beliefs independent of a church or synagogue.[3] This means that most Americans (and many others in Western culture) believe that the spiritual journey is primarily an individual

undertaking that emphasizes working independently on one's own faith synthesis.

In earlier social settings, individual autonomy was often balanced or even overshadowed by communal links with family and an ethnic group, both in close physical proximity, but today many individuals are more free from family and ethnic group influence. For example, in 1950 a young Irish woman in a tight-knit family living in a predominantly Irish area would take very seriously the opinions of her family and neighbors about a suitable marriage partner for her. In today's more mobile world, a young woman may act much more independently, for she frequently lives far from her immediate family and in a context where people of many different ethnic backgrounds live together.

3. *More elective ties to religious institutions:* Increased personal independence often, but not always, shows itself in looser ties to a religious institution. One sign of this relationship is the dramatic increase in switching denominations. Whereas a 1955 Gallup poll revealed that only 4 percent of adults in America had moved away from their childhood religious faith, in 1984 about 33 percent had switched.[4] Another sign is that more of those individuals who do affiliate with a church do so because they feel it will meet their needs. Belonging is based less upon common bonds with family, friends, or ethnic group, and more often upon a personal decision that a church will provide what one wants. Still another indication of how increased personal autonomy may affect bonds with a church is the increase in those who claim no affiliation with a religious institution. A 1947 Gallup poll showed 6 percent of Americans claimed no religious preference; in 1952 the number dropped to 2 percent, but by 1988 it had risen to 10 percent.[5] However, greater individual choice in religious affiliation does not always result in less commitment to a particular denomination, for in some cases personal choice of a denomination produces a deep commitment to a particular institution and tradition.

When individuals generally enjoy greater independence and, often, less attachment to a particular religious community, it is not surprising to find that in forming a personal faith synthesis they frequently combine elements from different spiritual or religious traditions. This is done with highly variable degrees of thoughtfulness and understanding of what is involved. On the one hand, already several decades ago, Thomas Merton, the well-known Roman Catholic monk and mystic, searched for common ground with Buddhist and Hindu monks and mystics while remaining deeply rooted in the Christian tradition. On the other hand, a recent study found that 14 percent of churchgoing (not fringe or inactive) Presbyterians affirmed belief in reincarnation, a belief common in Far Eastern and New Age religions but inconsistent with Christian teaching on resurrection.[6]

FOUR PATTERNS OF SPIRITUALITY

In this cultural context of increased religious pluralism, greater individual autonomy, and more elective ties to religious institutions, it is possible to distinguish four patterns in the way Americans relate to religious institutions as they pursue a spiritual journey.[7] These American patterns are very likely similar to those followed in other Western societies and may also have counterparts in other societies.

1. *Loyal Members—full commitment to a religious institution or tradition.* For those within Christianity, this means following the ways of worship, personal devotion, morality, and church organization of a certain denomination. For example, there are Roman Catholics who faithfully go to mass, express heartfelt devotion to the Virgin Mary, agree with the church's official moral teachings (maybe with the exception of birth control), and have deep respect for the church hierarchy. Similarly, there are Lutherans who regularly attend church, follow what they regard as a Christian ethic, join another Lutheran church when they move, and maybe have daily devotions with Scripture. Those who live out this pattern may have objections to this or that element of their religious tradition, but are largely satisfied with it. Some people become loyal members through lifelong immersion in the tradition; others arrive at it after experimentation and struggle.

2. *Loving Critics—selective commitment to a religious institution or tradition.* Those Christians who follow this pattern are loyal to a

denomination on their own terms. Although they have some serious dissatisfaction with the ways of this denomination and find spiritual nourishment in some other groups, they continue to identify with the denomination. For instance, there are charismatic Episcopalians who are active members of their denominational congregation. They probably have considered leaving the Episcopal church to join a Pentecostal church, but they have decided to remain Episcopalian. Outside their denominational structure, they participate in a charismatic prayer fellowship, go to ecumenical charismatic conferences, and sometimes attend special events at a Pentecostal church. There are loyal Lutherans who feel their church does not provide enough instruction and guidance in meditation, so they participate in some Roman Catholic-sponsored retreats on meditation and do some reading about Buddhist meditation. They have no intention of becoming Roman Catholic or Buddhist, yet they feel free to incorporate some Catholic and Buddhist practices into their spirituality. Similarly, there are African American Presbyterians who are troubled about ways in which their denomination is blind to racism and cultural diversity. Quite often at denominational gatherings, they feel they don't quite belong. Nevertheless, they remain loyal Presbyterians. When possible they gravitate toward predominantly black Presbyterian congregations where they can pray, sing, and hear preaching in the black tradition, and they are especially nurtured in African American fellowship groups. There are also many selective Roman Catholics, people who object, perhaps, to the patriarchal and hierarchical character of their church. Although they are often angry with the Roman Catholic Church, they stay within it. They still attend mass and believe there is a proper role for the papacy, but they want women priests and a less authoritarian church structure. They receive support in groups where feminism and mutuality are honored.

3. *Spiritual Shoppers—commitment to a religious institution or tradition to the extent that it contributes significantly to one's personal faith synthesis.* This relation to religious tradition is looser in two respects from the previous patterns. First, people who follow this pattern stay in a denomination or tradition only as long as they are

satisfied with what it provides. If they become dissatisfied or move to an area where a church of that denomination is not handy, they will switch to another denomination with little or no sense of loss. Denominational loyalty is considerably lower than in the former patterns. Also, individuals exhibit greater freedom in taking elements of belief and practice from widely diverse religious traditions to form their own synthesis of spirituality. They may combine certain Christian beliefs and practices with features from New Age, Hindu, and Native American religious traditions. The Presbyterians mentioned above as affirming belief in reincarnation exemplify this pattern of spirituality. Whereas those who have a selective commitment to a tradition clearly find the core of their spirituality in that tradition, those who follow this third pattern are more interested in forming their own spiritual blend. Sometimes they speak of "my God" and "your God" as though each person has his or her own deity or even that God is whatever a person believes about God.

4. *Independent Seekers—commitment above all to one's private faith development.* Those who exhibit this pattern of spirituality have only very loose connections with religious or spiritual organizations. They will participate in a group because they become interested in some aspects of its perspective and practice, but they tend to drift in and out. For example, they will attend some classes on yoga, but their relationship with the sponsoring organization is tenuous. Or they will read the gospels and sometimes come to worship at a church because they are drawn to the life and teachings of Jesus. They see themselves as not really belonging to any religious or spiritual organization. The focus is their individual faith development.

Three general observations about these four patterns are in order. First, people may stay in one of these patterns for life or may exhibit a different pattern at a different period of life. For example, as a teenager and single adult, one might be an independent seeker, as a young married person become a spiritual shopper, and as an older adult eventually become a loyal member of a church tradition. Or one might begin as a loyal member, experience disillusionment, and become an independent seeker. Second, any of these patterns can be lived out with varying degrees of thoughtfulness and self-awareness.

We should not assume that all loyal members are unreflective traditionalists simply afraid to leave a rut, nor should we think every independent seeker is a brave Socrates. Shoddy thinking and convention-bound living occur among those who follow each of the patterns, but in each there are also examples of careful thought and courageous living. Third, these four patterns represent segments of a wide spectrum of ways to relate to religious institutions. Since human beings do not fall neatly into categories, the reader may feel represented by more than one pattern or none at all.

The overall accuracy of this typology is confirmed by Princeton sociologist Robert Wuthnow in his study of spirituality in America. Wuthnow distinguishes what he calls a "spirituality of dwelling" from a "spirituality of seeking." In a *spirituality of dwelling,* God and one's relationship with God are rather confidently understood within the framework of symbols affirmed by a stable community of faith. This corresponds to what I call the stance of loyal members. Wuthnow's *spirituality of seeking* corresponds most fully to what I call independent seekers. Loving critics and spiritual shoppers occupy intermediate positions that combine, in varying degrees, elements of both dwelling and seeking. Wuthnow says the element of spiritual seeking, with its emphasis on personal choice among many options, has been dominant in the United States from the 1960s until almost the present, but it has frequently resulted in mere spiritual dabbling, no depth.

The relevance of Wuthnow's study for our purposes is that he argues what is needed now is a *practice-oriented spirituality,* that is, a spirituality centered in various intentional spiritual practices. Such a spirituality combines elements of both a dwelling spirituality and a seeking spirituality. On the one hand, someone with a practice oriented spirituality is commonly connected with a faith community that has time-tested spiritual practices and spiritual guides experienced in them. So a person dwells within a community and solid tradition and is not without spiritual roots. On the other hand, a practice-oriented spirituality also incorporates choice among various specific spiritual practices that are integrated into that tradition, not just a hodgepodge.[8] Wuthnow's approach agrees substantially with my own purpose in this book. I am convinced that the Lutheran tradition is solidly anchored in the gospel of Jesus Christ, emphasizes a core of practices that have a biblical promise to mediate that message, and has the freedom to incorporate other practices that are consistent with that gospel.

SPIRITUALITY

The recent surge of interest in spirituality reflects the contemporary Western cultural context with its emphases on pluralism, personal autonomy, and elective institutional ties. One's attitude toward "spirituality" corresponds roughly with one's assessment of these cultural forces. We can distinguish three major attitudes.

1. *There is the attitude that spirituality is good, religion is bad.* For example, it is common to hear someone say, "I'm a spiritual person, but I'm not religious." Religion here is equated with "organized religion," which is understood negatively as an empty shell of habit, ritual, and organization with little inner life. In contrast, spirituality is understood positively as belonging to the individual's own experience. Spirituality tends to be regarded as an unambiguous good. The "I'm spiritual but not religious" sentiment is most often expressed by the independent seeker who strongly endorses individual autonomy, loose ties with religious institutions, and spiritual pluralism.

There are many authors, speakers, and groups that pitch their message to this audience of seekers. For example, Thomas Moore, author of the best-seller *Care of the Soul* and other books, addresses chiefly those who are forming their own faith synthesis. He says, "Spiritual practice is sometimes described as walking in the footsteps of another: Jesus is the way, the truth, and the life; the bodhisattva's life models the way. But on the soul's odyssey, or in its labyrinth, the feeling is that no one has ever gone this way before."[9] Thomas Moore himself models the sort of person who does not clearly identify with any one religious tradition, but borrows freely from a variety of traditions. Perhaps it's not surprising that the basic framework of his outlook actually originates in Jungian psychology rather than a religious tradition.

2. *In the second attitude toward spirituality, religion and spirituality are not contrasted so sharply.* For instance, when asked what he means

by "spiritual life," Yale philosopher of religion Louis Dupre replied, "A religious life built upon an attitude of personal response to the call of the divine. Such an attitude originates *within the self*: it is not derived from the force of inherited habits nor from people's tendency to yield to social pressure."[10] According to Louis Dupre, one can be both religious and spiritual, so there is a more positive evaluation of religious institutions. However, the distinctive emphasis of "spiritual" is personal response. Spirituality belongs to a person's own experience; it's not just a matter of inherited habits or social pressure. Here the element of personal autonomy may appear within the realm of religion. This closer relation between religion and spirituality is evident in the fact that many contemporary loyal members, loving critics of churches, and spiritual shoppers are searching for the inner life or spirituality of Christian traditions. Such people actively participate in "organized religion," but they are not satisfied with a merely routine religious life. They want to be awake to God's presence and call.

3. *Another attitude toward spirituality is seen in those theologians and church leaders who see it as a dangerous slough into which Christians ought not venture.* The cultural forces of increased personal autonomy, elective institutional ties, and pluralism are viewed largely as threats stemming from an exaggerated individualism. What is called spirituality is regarded as a jumble of ideas with little Christian content; it is simply another way human beings create their own views of God. Like the ancient Israelites in the desert who constructed idols out of gold, people today, under the guise of spirituality, are building images of God to suit their liking. Consequently these theologians and church leaders regard "spirituality" as evil or highly suspect.

My own view is closest to the second perspective, for I think "spirituality" is neither unambiguously good nor unambiguously evil, but is just as mixed a reality as the phenomena of religion or faith. On the positive side, the term *spirituality* is a useful way of talking about the ways we human spirits transcend our immediate circumstances and ask about a larger reality and meaning. A spirituality is the way that a person or group answers the question and lives out that answer in various practices.

So, *a spirituality* is a *lived faith* plus *a path*. Let's examine each part of this definition. First, in actual life there is no such thing as generic spirituality; there are only specific spiritualities. Hence I speak here of *a* spirituality.

Second, a spirituality always involves a particular lived faith. Faith is sometimes a fuzzy word, but I think faith includes at least three elements: commitment, belief, and trust. (a) While we have many commitments (to meet someone for lunch, fulfill certain duties at work, etc.), the commitment that belongs to a person's faith is one's *highest commitment*. It is that commitment that takes priority over every other commitment. (b) Faith also includes *belief,* which means claiming something to be true. We also have many beliefs; for instance, we hold it as true that we exist in a solar system that includes planets named Jupiter and Uranus. However, such beliefs probably are not relevant to one's highest commitment. The beliefs that belong to a person's faith are those that together form a picture of reality within which that person's highest commitment makes sense. For example, someone who gives his or her highest commitment to God does so within a worldview that includes the belief that God exists. Someone whose ultimate commitment is to the Communist Party has a cluster of beliefs that view the party as the main engine in human history. (c) The third element of faith is *trust.* Here we rely upon something, have confidence in it. Again, we trust a great many things. We trust the chair on which we are now sitting to hold us up, and in varying degrees we trust some other people and also ourselves. The trust that belongs to a person's faith is the person's most basic trust. So one's real faith is determined not by membership in a religious organization, but by identifying what is one's highest commitment and in what one places one's ultimate trust. The relevant beliefs constitute a worldview within which this ultimate commitment and trust make sense.

Since faith is an integral element of spirituality, any spirituality that involves belief in God will also include a *theology,* that is, a particular interpretation of God and how human beings are related to God. In fact, different schools of Christian spirituality are closely connected with different theologies. Yet spirituality involves a *lived* faith, not just a theory. That is, faith here does not indicate merely a set of doctrines or beliefs, nor just membership in a certain institution or school of thought. Rather, spirituality refers to actual experience of faith that has a particular configuration of commitment, trust, and belief.

I've said that a spirituality equals a lived faith plus a path. By "path" I mean a holistic way in which a particular faith is nurtured and expressed. This customarily includes certain practices, rituals, group participation, moral behavior, and teachings. Someone adopts and lives the faith of Wicca or witchcraft through reading about it, participating in various rituals, such as a new moon ritual, and being part of a coven whose members support one another.[11]

There is considerable overlap between "spirituality" and "religion," for religion includes certain teachings, rituals, and practices in which people express a certain faith and are nurtured in that faith. Thus I do not think there is usually a wide gulf between religion and spirituality. In fact, I think *spirituality* is most often another name for religion. But in our contemporary situation where many people see religion as merely formal and external, the term *spirituality* suggests "real, lived religion" or "real, lived faith." So *spirituality* is a useful word today, since it conveys the sense of a faith that is part of one's own daily life and experience.

So far we've looked at the positive aspects of the term spirituality. On the negative side, much of what is represented under the title of spirituality are ways in which we human beings try to manage our relationship with God. Rather than trust in God's merciful goodness, we trust in our own wisdom and strength. The whole idea of the individual embarking on some heroic quest for self-fulfillment is fundamentally a selfish notion in which the self becomes the center of everything. To treat anything in this world as the center of all is the essence of idolatry, treating a creature as though it were God. But the same criticism applies to much that is presented as religion, faith, or Christianity. In the end, genuine spirituality (or genuine religion, faith, or Christianity) is not so much our creation as it is the gift of God. In Christian terms, wholesome, healing spirituality is a gift of the Holy Spirit working within the human spirit.[12]

TRADITIONS OF CHRISTIAN SPIRITUALITY

In our search for a faith that is integral to our daily life and experience, it is wise to consult traditions of spirituality. It is foolish to ignore the insights and wisdom that others have gained and passed on from generation to generation. Many people in Western societies believe that Eastern religious traditions are more "pure," but that is simply because those traditions are less familiar. All religious traditions have their bumps and warts. To overlook Christianity is to miss a great treasure.

In Christianity many traditions are identified with a particular denomination; one can speak of Methodist spirituality, Reformed spirituality, Catholic spirituality, or Lutheran spirituality. However, each of these spiritualities is really a family of spirituality that includes subtypes. For example, within the family of Catholic spirituality, there are Benedictine, Franciscan, Ignatian, and other forms of spirituality. In this book we will focus on the Lutheran tradition and gain some understanding of the diversity of subspiritualities that have existed, and still exist, within that family.

First, it will be helpful to locate the Lutheran tradition within Christianity. Like every other great religion, Christianity has formed different families, often called denominations. While we will concentrate on Lutheranism, we should not forget that it is related in various ways to other Christian families. This is a very simplified diagram of these families:

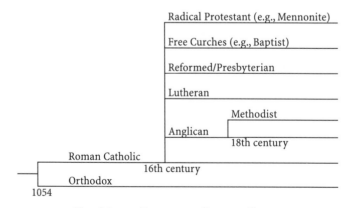

THE MAJOR CHRISTIAN CHURCH FAMILIES

Just as we as individuals are influenced by our life experiences, so the Lutheran family has been shaped by its historical development. I shall call attention to some high points in this rich family history.

A SKETCH OF THE LUTHERAN FAMILY HISTORY

1. *The Lutheran Reformation.* The initial impetus for the Reformation was Martin Luther's personal quest for peace with God. Although Luther became a monk and then a university professor who lectured on the Bible, he did not find peace with God. Luther tells us that the dominant theology of his day taught him to think of God as a strict judge and that salvation comes through a combination of God's grace and human effort. Luther was painfully aware that divine grace had not totally transformed him, for sin still influenced his thoughts and actions. So his deep personal question was this: If God is a strict judge and I am still only a partially transformed sinner, how can I be confident that God accepts me?

Over several years of studying the Bible, especially Paul's letters, Luther found his answer: the gospel of Jesus Christ tells us that God is not a strict judge, but is loving and merciful toward those who trust in God. Luther's understanding of grace is commonly called "justification by grace through faith" or simply "justification by faith." This teaching, and the underlying concern about peace with God, have been persistent themes in Lutheranism.

Luther's understanding of justification took on wider significance when he publicly criticized certain church teachings and practices concerning penance and indulgences. On October 31, 1517, Luther publicly posted ninety-five theses in Latin for academic discussion of indulgences. The theses were quite conservative, for in them Luther only questioned some abuses of indulgences and did not reject them entirely. Much to his surprise, though, a storm erupted. His theses were quickly translated into German and circulated widely. Although authorities in Rome and elsewhere opposed Luther, his call for reform soon broadened: the authority of Scripture is above that of popes and church councils, there are two or three rather than seven sacraments, and in the Lord's supper the laity should receive wine as well as bread.

Although Luther was excommunicated by the pope and con-
demned to death by the Holy Roman Emperor, he was protected by
his territorial prince. The Lutheran reform movement spread quickly through most of northern Germany and soon prevailed in Denmark, Norway, Sweden, and Finland. Since Lutheran views were
vigorously opposed by church and civil authorities in southern and
eastern Europe, and had far less success than other reform movements in Switzerland, Netherlands, France, and Britain, Lutheranism
took hold almost entirely in northern Europe. Luther and his supporters did not set out to establish a separate church. They started a
movement intended merely to reform Roman Catholic Christianity.
Repeated efforts on both sides attempted to heal the breach. One of
the most significant was at Augsburg, Germany, in 1530. Since Luther
was an outlaw unable to travel safely in Roman Catholic territory, his
close associate Philip Melanchthon was the chief author of a formulation of Lutheran teachings in the Augsburg Confession. When
Luther died in 1546, the Lutheran reform movement had formed a
cluster of precarious regional churches separated from the Roman
Catholic Church, although there were still those who tried to reunify
the church either through reconciliation or compulsion.

2. *Lutheran orthodoxy.* It is common with social movements that
the fresh insights of the first generation give way to the desire to preserve what has been achieved. This happened to the Lutheran reform
movement. After Luther died, disputes arose over the proper understanding of certain teachings. Melanchthon's tendency to take somewhat different positions than Luther added fuel to the conflicts.
Melanchthon's death in 1560 left the next generation of German
Lutheran theologians to work through the differences. The fruit of
their labors was the Formula of Concord (1577). A further sign of
consolidation happened when this document, along with the Augsburg Confession, Apology to the Augsburg Confession, Luther's Small
and Large Catechisms, and the Smalcald Articles, were published as
the *Book of Concord* (1580). Since these documents formed a doctrinal standard for German Lutheran Churches, they are called the
Lutheran confessions. The church in Denmark and Norway accepted
just the Augsburg Confession and Luther's Small Catechism, while

the church in Sweden and Finland later acknowledged the entire *Book of Concord* but gave primacy to the Augsburg Confession.

It is important to note that Lutheranism has been a tradition in which Christian doctrine is taken very seriously. Starting in 1580, Lutheran orthodox theologians made doctrine even more prominent when they sought to preserve Luther's views by producing orderly and detailed presentations of Lutheran doctrine that combatively argued its superiority to other teachings. The heyday of Lutheran orthodoxy was over by the mid-1700s, but its spirit lives on yet today. Whereas some Christians emphasize what various believers hold in common and may even downplay doctrinal differences, the Lutheran orthodox spirit considers it vital to have detailed agreement on points of doctrine.

3. *Lutheran pietism.* Pietism as a religious movement began in 1675, but many of its themes were sounded earlier by John Arndt in his widely used devotional book, *True Christianity* (first published in 1605). Whereas Luther's primary concern was to assure people weighed down by rules and guilt that God is merciful, Arndt felt that many who had lived all their lives under Lutheranism were taking God's mercy for granted and living unchanged lives. So Arndt emphasized repentance and transformation of life through Christ present in the believer. Arndt's themes were picked up by Philip Spener, whose book *Pia Desideria* (1675) set in motion pietism as a religious movement that influenced many Lutherans in Germany and Scandinavia. Several features characterized pietists at that time: (1) meeting in small groups called "conventicles" to discuss the Bible and pray, (2) encouragement of lay leadership, (3) a rigorous moral life that often prohibited card playing, dancing, and alcohol, (4) initiation of Lutheran missionary work outside Europe.

The pietist movement fostered a different form of Lutheran spirituality than orthodoxy. What is central for the pietist is the experience of a personal faith in Jesus that manifests itself in a highly moral life and public witness to others. Doctrine is not unimportant, but pietist leaders wrote devotional books, not formal theology. Whereas Lutheran orthodox leaders stressed the differences of Lutheran doctrine from that of other churches, pietist spiritual writers borrowed freely from Roman Catholic and Reformed sources that the orthodox regarded as suspect.

Nevertheless, Lutheran pietism and Lutheran orthodoxy share some things. They both look to Luther and the Lutheran confessions. They also share a devotion to a number of hymns such as those by Philipp Nicolai and Paul Gerhardt.[13]

Pietism and orthodoxy have remained through the centuries enduring influences on Lutheran spirituality even as they have blended at times with each other and with other currents in religion and culture. For example, during the eighteenth century a new cultural movement called the Enlightenment grew in Europe and America. The bent of Enlightenment thinkers such as Americans Benjamin Franklin and Thomas Jefferson was to rely upon reason rather than Scripture as the standard of truth in religion and morality. Many traditional Christian teachings were set aside, so that Jesus was regarded merely as model of the moral life, not as Savior from sin. Partly in response to such thinking, a religious awakening occurred throughout Lutheranism in the late eighteenth and early nineteenth centuries. The awakening took various forms. In some cases, there was a resurgence of concern for sound Lutheran doctrine as in orthodoxy. A similar concern is evident today in those Lutherans who are wary of the instability of religious experience and stress reliance on the objective word of God. In other cases, pietism was revitalized in movements led by Hauge in Norway and Rosenius in Sweden. One fruit of this Lutheran awakening was strong support for mission work both within the homeland (called Inner Mission) and abroad through various foreign mission societies.

Recent pietist patterns of spirituality are seen in those Lutherans cordial toward Evangelicalism and the charismatic movement. Many Lutherans have been drawn to the Evangelicalism of Billy Graham and others who stress a personal conversion experience in which one is said to be born again. Another pietist pattern of spirituality is charismatic Lutheranism, which, in addition to requiring a conscious decision of faith in Jesus, accentuates a second experience called baptism in the Holy Spirit.

There have been other types of Lutheran spirituality not borne of orthodoxy and pietism. Some Lutherans have been contemplators, others have been social activists, still others have been devoted to liturgy. On top of such variations of spirituality come also differences in culture, so the Lutheranism of African Americans in Chicago is distinct from the Lutheranism of Finnish Americans in the Upper Peninsula of Michigan, and both are different from the Lutheranism of El Salvador. There are many possibilities. What they all have in common is engagement with the Lutheran tradition, especially the Lutheran confessions and Martin Luther. This engagement with the Lutheran tradition acts like the genetic and social heritage of a family that produces family members who resemble one another. For example, children of the same parents generally resemble their parents and also one another, but they are not identical. They have similar physical characteristics such as an extra long nose, and they share certain behavioral patterns that are alike. In similar fashion, engagement with the Lutheran tradition tends to produce spiritualities that constitute a family with certain shared characteristics.

I believe the Lutheran family of spirituality has these seven characteristics:

1. Conviction that alienation from God is the deep and persistent root of our problems as individuals and communities.

2. Trust that God's merciful grace undergirds all of life.

3. Reliance on the word of God in Scripture, proclamation, and music as the primary source of spiritual nurture and guidance.

4. Confidence that God's grace is present in the sacraments of baptism and the Lord's supper and may also work through other rites, gestures, and physical objects.

5. Participation in the communal life of the church with responsibility for the nurture of one another.

6. Deep loyalty to core church traditions as expressed in the classic creeds and Lutheran confessions and both respect and freedom toward secondary traditions.

7. Conviction that God's twofold rule summons all people to seek justice and calls Christians to faithful service in their daily relationships in life.

While other Christian spiritual traditions may share in one or several of these characteristics, only Lutheran spirituality manifests all seven of them. In each of the next seven chapters, we will examine one of these characteristics of Lutheran spirituality.

My aim in this book is to foster spiritual dialogue and growth on several levels. On one level, we will be in dialogue with the Lutheran tradition in Christianity, so that we may grow in our understanding of it. On another level, we will engage in conversation and debate with one another about strengths and weaknesses of the Lutheran tradition. On the deepest level, though, the intention is to be in dialogue with God through reflection and spiritual exercise. Our look at Lutheran spirituality is not simply for the purpose of filling your memory with more information, although we will need to discuss some ideas and facts about Lutheranism. The intent is also to provide occasions for you to ponder your relationship with God and how that relationship may be strengthened through a range of possible spiritual practices.

FOR REFLECTION AND PRACTICE

1. How would you characterize yourself now: loyal member, loving critic, spiritual shopper, independent seeker, or something else? How would you characterize yourself during earlier stages in your life?

2. What is your own attitude toward the term *spirituality?* Do you agree with one of the three attitudes identified in the third section of this chapter; is the term new to you; is the term simply neutral for you, or do you have some other point of view?

3. What has been your relationship with and attitude toward the Lutheran tradition?

If these questions are used with a group, it will be most fruitful if individuals are given some time alone to reflect on the first question before joining together for sharing in small groups of three to five, and then coming together as a whole group. The second and third questions could be raised in small groups first.

2

OUR HUMAN CONDITION

McDOUGLE WAS A WONDERFUL DOG who shared the life of our family for thirteen years. He was the runt of a litter of Pekipoos—half Pekingese, half poodle. McDougle was an affectionate dog who always greeted arriving family members with a wagging tail and a glad-to-see-you look. The high points of his day were a morning and evening walk that he devoted mostly to sniffing at trees and leaving his scent all along the route. The rest of his time was spent largely in sleep, especially as he grew older. I suspect McDougle had a very good canine life; he had plenty of food, a warm bed, and affection. As far as I can tell, though, McDougle never reflected on his life and asked whether his existence in the Hanson household was all there was available to a dog. He never asked whether he might rather go off to Hollywood to pursue a career in film or explore outer space with NASA. It does not appear that a dog has the capability to ask such questions.

We human beings do ask questions about the direction and meaning of our own existence as well as questions about the meaning of the world we inhabit. Our capacity as spiritual beings enables us to stand outside our immediate circumstances and ask about their meaning. Like every other living thing on earth, we are on a journey from birth to death. We wonder, though, whether there is more to our journey than that. We are wayfarers who must chart a course, yet it is not obvious what direction we should take. We are seekers looking for signs to help us find our way.

Our situation is further complicated by the fact that we ourselves seem flawed in some ways. That is, our difficulty in charting and following a course in life is not caused merely by natural limits in power and intelligence. We all have had the experience of believing we should follow a certain path yet not carrying through. As we look back over our life, we see personal actions that we regret, some of them with deep pain. And when we look outward at society, we see much that is wrong: murders, wars, terrible addictions, abuse, child neglect. The list goes on and on. The signs that human life is not what it might be are so widespread that every religion and philosophy of life offers some explanation for the human predicament. So must we who are seeking to find our way. An important step in taking a major journey is an honest, searching appraisal of our own condition.

In our appraisal, we must answer three questions about our human condition: (1) What are we meant to be? (2) What has gone wrong? (3) What is needed to set things right? We shall consider each question in the light of Christian faith and the Lutheran tradition in the hope that this dialogue will help you sort out your own thinking on these important issues.

WHAT ARE WE MEANT TO BE?

In order to set a course, we must have a destination or goal. Of course, we have many goals—goals for today, this week, this year, or maybe the next ten years. The goal of which I speak is the one that is above all the others: What is the ultimate goal or purpose of my life? One might say, "I just want to be happy." Of course, all of us want to be happy. Indeed, it's unlikely that anyone consciously wants to be unhappy. But is happiness the fundamental purpose of one's life? What if one suffers a serious loss that makes one unhappy? Is one's basic purpose in life taken away? Or is there a purpose more fundamental?

Another way to look at these questions is to ask what should be our first priority. As we noted in the previous chapter, we all have many commitments—a commitment to meet someone for lunch tomorrow, a responsibility to get something done by the end of the week, various commitments to family members. But what is our highest commitment, our most important priority? Our highest priority is what establishes the fundamental direction of our life. Does our highest priority *deserve* to be first? Is it worthy of being our ultimate commitment?

These are hard questions to ask, but they are the most vital, because they urge us to reflect on the course of our life and clarify our fundamental purpose. It may be difficult to articulate our actual fundamental purpose. What may feel the most real are near-at-hand goals like do well in school, be happy in my marriage, get my kids on their feet, do my work well, make it through this illness. While such goals are indeed good, are they durable enough to be our ultimate purpose in life? Here dialogue with Christian faith and the Lutheran tradition may be fruitful.

According to a Christian understanding, our fundamental goal in life is to be genuinely free persons whose hearts are devoted to God and caring toward other people and creatures. First and most basic, we are meant to be *persons whose hearts are devoted to God*. Our hearts do in fact have a central devotion, something or someone that matters most of all to us. This center is what we care about most of all, what we love above all else. The biblical approach to devotion says that our heart should find its center in God. This notion is expressed as a command in the Old Testament and Jesus affirms it in the New Testament, "You shall love the Lord your God with all your heart, and with all your soul, and with all your mind" (Deuteronomy 6:5; Matthew 22:37).

The core devotion of our heart establishes the underlying direction of our life. Imagine that money is at the center of my heart. That makes money my first priority, my highest commitment. It's what I care about most of all, what I love most. Of course, I'll have other commitments, say, to family. But my commitments to family will always take second place to money whenever the two come into conflict. As my chief priority, money will take precedence over other priorities. Thus my life has an overall direction in and through its many turns.

Scripture holds that only God deserves to be the center of our heart. Only God deserves to be our primary priority. To have anything else as our highest commitment is idolatry, worship of a creature rather than God. The core act of worship is not some ritual done in a church or other sanctuary. We worship all the time by giving our fundamental devotion to something. The question to ask ourselves is, What is it that I care about most of all? The biblical view is that our lives are properly balanced when God is our heart's center. Then we have enduring stability and peace.

Second, we are meant to be *persons whose hearts are caring toward other people and creatures.* The main emphasis of Scripture is on caring for other people. Jesus follows rabbinic custom in summarizing Jewish law when he declares the second great commandment: "You shall love your neighbor as yourself" (Matthew 22:39). Love for neighbor does not mean to have a deep emotional attachment such as we may have to family members, nor does it mean to have romantic feelings. To love our neighbor is to seek his or her best interest, to strive for that person's well-being. Jesus illustrated such love in the story of a Jewish man traveling in a dangerous area who was robbed and severely beaten. Later one Jewish religious leader and then another passed by the injured man without helping, and then a Samaritan (Jews and Samaritans were hostile toward one another) came by, bandaged his wounds, and took him to an inn where he could mend (Luke 10:29-37). It was the Samaritan who cared for his neighbor.

Further, we are meant to care for other creatures. Such care is indicated in several of the earliest stories of the Bible. In the creation story of Genesis, chapter 1, humans are given dominion over other creatures, but the context makes clear that this is to be a dominion like God's own—one marked by concern for what is different. The creation account in Genesis 2 reinforces this with the understanding that the first human was put in the garden of Eden as its steward or caretaker. Then, after the great flood, God makes the first covenant not only with humans but also with "every living creature" (Genesis 9:10). Since God values every living creature, we are meant to have hearts that also care for them.

Third, we are meant to be *genuinely free persons.* One might ask, Are we not innately free? Yes, in some respects we are innately free, for we have the ability to choose among many alternatives. Yet personal experience and observation tell us that we human beings often make choices that are damaging to others and to ourselves. The apostle Paul and the Lutheran tradition teach that a more authentic freedom is to willingly choose the good. Their claim is that when we love God and love others, we also truly love ourself and are genuinely free.

Altogether, Scripture sets forth a simple yet profound vision of what human beings are meant to be. Fundamental is a heart centrally devoted to God. This provides the basic direction of life. No doubt there are a number of worthy values to affirm—family, community, justice, knowledge, beauty, and health, to name a few. Each of these values shares something in common with God. Nevertheless, when worshiped independently of God, these values finally disappoint. For instance, family can be lost, community can become perverse, and justice can lack mercy. Such values were not meant to bear the weight of taking God's place. When something other than God is the center of our heart, then our life becomes unbalanced. It lacks enduring stability and peace.

A heart centrally devoted to God is naturally open to other people and creatures, for God's love is inclusive. We are not intended to pass our days with eyes only on heaven. Neither does God want us to live with hearts bent only on the safety and comfort of ourselves and those closest to us. A what's-in-it-for-me attitude may help make us successful in the world, but it also turns us into cramped human beings. Generosity and compassion are the marks of full persons.

There is little doubt that if we all had hearts devoted to God and open to others, the world would be a wonderful place. But experience tells us that life is not as it should be. Attention to our own feelings makes us aware of fears, regrets, and resentments that are clues to something awry. Relationships with family members, friends, and coworkers often have a dark side. When we look further, it is obvious that we humans fall far short in caring for one another. People begging on the street, sensational killings that make the front page, fear of being attacked or robbed, abuse of children and women, and great inequality of wealth in the world are just a few symptoms that something is wrong. There are a great many symptoms, but what is the underlying problem? This is a question that every religion, spirituality, or view of life must address.

What Has Gone Wrong?

There are many answers to this question; they come from popular culture, psychology, various philosophies, and religions. Some elements of popular culture suggest that what is wrong is either lack of communication or not taking time to think before we act. To be sure, the world would be more wholesome if we communicated better with one another and consistently thought carefully before we acted, but it is very doubtful that these answers get at the basic problem. Others say money is the root of all evil. But would the world be significantly better if we somehow banished money from earth? People would just be greedy for something else. Is greed, then, the root of evil? Certainly it is a major flaw, but greed does not seem to apply to many conflicts, say, between spouses.

Modern social, political, and psychological theories have spawned some influential explanations of what has gone wrong in human life. One set of suggestions finds the fundamental flaw in unjust social arrangements along economic, gender, or racial lines. Social transformation, maybe revolutionary change, is then regarded as the key to future gain. Another group of answers comes from psychological theories that commonly identify the problems of society with negative social influences that distort the innate goodness of individuals and stifle their potential. Another powerful proposal in Western culture is that our chief weakness is ignorance, the kind of ignorance that could be banished through advancements in objective knowledge like that in science.

The suggestion that underlies the wide range of New Age leaders and groups focuses on a more personal kind of ignorance. This ignorance is an underdeveloped consciousness, rather than a lack of information. According to a common New Age outlook, there is a spark of the divine in all of us, and we are meant to be one with God and the rhythms of nature. In fact, at bottom God is felt to be one with the world and the world one with God. In our ignorance, however, we do not realize our destiny to experience unity with all things nor our innate potential to reach it. We get mired down in merely technical knowledge and control of nature. The churches mislead people by training them to be obedient "believers" of doctrines. What we need, say many New Age leaders, are reliable guides to help us acquire genuine knowledge by raising our consciousness. Right now I am looking at a flyer advertising a number of New Age events intended to achieve a higher level of awareness. Included are an equinox ritual that employs "magic," an evening devoted to reading

Tarot cards, and a session on regression to one's previous lives in the cycle of reincarnation. The basic aim is to lift people out of an under-developed consciousness.

There are varying degrees of insight in these diverse proposals of what is wrong in human life. None are entirely without merit, yet it would be imprudent to ignore what Scripture says about our condi-tion. Christian faith and the Lutheran tradition say the most funda-mental flaw in human existence is a breakdown in our relationship with God. The breakdown is more like *alienation between friends* than ignorance. If our heart were devoted to God, we would trust and love him with all our heart.[1] God would be our very best friend, the one to whom we would turn in every time of need and on whom we would rely in every situation. As it is, though, we are distanced in var-ious ways from our divine friend. Rather than trust completely, we are cautious, maybe even skeptical, about letting God into our life. Rather than a wholehearted love, our heart is divided; any love we have for our divine friend competes with and often loses out to all sorts of other affections. The result is that our relationship with God suffers alienation.

The core Christian view is that alienation from God is not just a disturbance in a peripheral area while the rest of life can function very well indeed. Alienation from God has negative effects through-out every facet of life. This makes sense if we remember that, from a Christian perspective, our hearts are meant to be centered on God. That is, God is meant to be the center around which everything revolves. Genuine faith in God, not a pseudofaith dressed in religios-ity or patriotism, brings order, strength, durability, and peace to all realms of life. The proper balance has been found. A God-centered heart brings balance to the self and greater care for others. The self finds steadiness and joy in a freedom grounded in God, which is both beyond and within the self. Family, work, friends, and community responsibilities find their appropriate places.

When something other than God becomes our center, then every-thing is changed. Yet life does not fall apart. We may still love our families, do our work, and help out a friend or neighbor. But without a heart centered in God, we wobble through life. We may or may not fall down, but in any case we are unsteady. The self loses the solid ground on which genuine human freedom is established. Some people go the way of a spurious freedom in which the *inflated self* makes itself the center around which all should revolve; one seeks to dominate and control other people and nature. Others experience in various degrees a *depleted self;* although outwardly one may be coping well, inwardly one feels empty, low, insignificant. The depleted self feels trapped by forces within the family, larger society, nature, and even itself—forces that rob it of value and meaning. One longs for a loving other who would affirm one's worth. When one is distanced from that love, one feels empty. Alienation from God means separation from the only love that is always reliable. Alienation from God brings about estrangement within the self and distortion in relationships with other people and nature.

One might wonder whether alienation from God could have such a powerful effect on one's life unless one previously had a deep faith in God. It seems reasonable that if highly religious persons have a strong belief in God and act contrary to that belief, then they would feel alienated from a friend and out of balance. But it might not seem to matter to those for whom God is a distant acquaintance or even unknown. How can you miss what you do not value? We can see examples of this, though, in other realms of life. In nutrition, people may be afflicted with a vitamin or mineral deficiency without realizing what they are missing. In social relations, persons may suffer from a lack of love, but themselves not recognize what is wrong. Similarly, Christian faith says that being distant from God has an adverse effect on all aspects of life, whether one realizes it or not.

This applies also to society. Not only are individual people flawed, but human groups are affected by the condition of sin. Injustice, crime, grave inequality, domination, and abuse become institutionalized in social patterns that persist over generations. The nineteenth and twentieth centuries have witnessed efforts to produce the good society through various efforts at social reform. Gains have been achieved in areas such as the abolition of slavery, regulation of child labor, and care for the mentally ill. Nevertheless, new social problems such as widespread drug addiction and weapons of mass destruction have also appeared. The symptoms of sin in society have changed somewhat, but it would be foolish to claim that the underlying condition has been banished. So it is that every human being is born into a family, local community, and world society that are deeply flawed by the condition of sin. In good part, this is what Christians mean when they talk about *original sin*. Because the situation into which we come is so flawed, each one of us is affected by the condition and our self also finds its center in something other than God.

The opening three chapters of the Bible testify to the centrality of our relationship with God. The very first chapter gives an account of creation in which humans are created "in the image of God" (Genesis 1:27). This doesn't mean that humans literally look like God, but metaphorically it suggests that we are meant to have a unique relationship with God. There is special communication between God and humans as well as responsibility to God. In the creation story of the second chapter, God shows touching solicitude for the good of the first human by creating a suitable partner. In the third chapter about the fall of humanity from paradise, the key is the relationship of humans with God. The breach with God is first signaled by lack of trust in the Creator and then openly manifested in disobedience and fear of God. What was meant to be a friendship between a senior and a junior has suffered estrangement. Significant also in Genesis 3 are signs of alienation in the self as well as in the relationship between humans and between humans and nature. After breaking trust with God, the first humans experience the self-alienation of shame over their nakedness. Their relationship with one another is broken when they blame one another, and soon the man begins to subordinate the woman. Distortions in the human relation with nature also are suggested in the story by the enmity established between people and snakes and the hindrances people will face in tilling soil. These opening chapters of the Bible need not be considered literal, historical accounts, for their claim to truth lies in identifying both what humans are meant to be and the comprehensive alienation that distorts human life.

The central Christian word for this total alienation is *sin*. Unfortunately, sin is often trivialized by narrowing it to particular acts of wrongdoing such as theft, drunkenness, and adultery. More basic than particular sins (plural) is the underlying *condition of sin*. This distinction is similar to that between specific symptoms of a disease such as cancer and the underlying condition of cancer. It's not enough merely to moderate the symptoms; it's the fundamental condition that is the root of the problem. So it is with sin. To alter this or that expression of sin without attending to the underlying condition is merely scratching the surface.

As we have seen in Genesis 3, the basic sin is lack of faith in God. Faith consists essentially of trust in and commitment to God. To have such faith is to have a heart centered in God. The condition of sin is to trust more in something other than God and to care more about it. Thus the essence of sin consists in a fundamental orientation of the self. To try to change a particular bad behavior without attending to the underlying orientation of the self is like treating a symptom and ignoring the disease. Twelve Step programs such as Alcoholics Anonymous recognize this to some extent in dealing with an addiction, for the program begins by turning to a higher power. The Christian tradition says the same principle applies with all the particular sins involving relations of humans with one another and with nature. The basic problem is that the self is not centrally devoted to God; the self is oriented away from God.

This raises an important question: How may the self be reoriented to trust in God? In other words, how may things be set right?

What is Needed to Set Things Right?

How we answer this question about setting things right is correlated with what we believe has gone wrong. If the human flaw is lack of communication, then better communication is the way to set things right. If ignorance of objective knowledge is the core problem, then improved education in the natural and social sciences is the answer. When Christian faith says that the root of our difficulties is that the self is centered in some creature rather than in the Creator, what we need is a basic reorientation of the self. How may this happen?

Answers to this question differ. Indeed, within the Christian tradition itself, there have been significantly different answers. It will help us to distinguish three views.

1. *Since we are slow learners, God shows us the way and we are able to follow.* This outlook holds that God shows people the way to live through ethical teachings such as the Ten Commandments. We are able to follow these teachings and examples, but often we do not.

People are sidetracked by bad examples and get caught in bad habits. Nevertheless, with sincere desire we are able to turn our lives in the right direction. Although the persistent influence of bad habits and negative social pressures prevent us from following God's will perfectly, at least we are able to make the basic reorientation of our life toward God. A proponent of this position in Christian history was a monk named Pelagius who, in the early fourth century B.C.E., advanced ideas like this. Part of his reasoning was "If I ought, then I can." That is, if God sets forth teachings that we ought to follow, then we must be able to do so.

A contemporary version of this perspective holds that there is a core of morality underlying all the religions and spiritualities, and the key is to follow that morality reasonably well. The various religions and spiritualities are diverse ways in which people interpret God. Like patrons at a buffet of spiritual entrées, we may pick religious or spiritual offerings that appeal most to us. What really counts, though, is that we follow "fundamental" morality.

2. *Since we are weak, God helps us have faith, but we must do our part.* In this view, there is a strong emphasis on the active love of God that seeks the lost. We can never set things right on our own, for in our weakness we get overly attached to other things. God must help, and more help is needed than moral instruction and good examples. God goes further by trying to persuade us through the gospel message to give our trust and commitment to God. Nevertheless, God respects our free will and leaves it up to us to accept or reject the divine offer. To center one's trust and love in God is the biggest decision of a person's life. While this view is generally supported by Christian television evangelists, it is also widely held. It agrees with what most people today would call common sense, in part because we tend to believe we have free will in all matters and in part because many Christians are conscious of having made a commitment to Christ.

3. *Since we are distrustful, God's faithful presence enables us to trust God.* This outlook is the most difficult to understand, for it runs counter to the powerful cultural conviction that we have free will in all matters. Yet this is the view held by the Lutheran confessional

writings as well as by Martin Luther and the three other greatest theologians in Western Christianity—Augustine, Thomas Aquinas, and John Calvin. The fact that all these theological heavyweights favor this position should prompt us to pause and consider it carefully.

This is a basic point: Reorienting the self toward God operates on a different level than everyday choices. We can see analogies to this in our ordinary experience. For example, remember a time when you were very worried about something. Someone may have said to you, "Don't worry," or "Try not to worry." Yet you found that you could not stop worrying. The point is that worry is not something we can choose to do or not do. Worry is not subject to volition or choice. Worry and confidence seem to emerge from a deeper level of the self. So also does putting faith in God.

Another example more closely relates the point to faith in God. Imagine an eight-year-old girl who has been abandoned by her parents and then passed from one family member to another and physically and sexually abused by some of them. Now the girl does not trust anyone. Life experience has taught her that the only person she can rely upon is herself. At this juncture you enter the picture as someone who wants to help her. You want to be a true friend to her. So you say to the girl, "Trust me." The question is whether she is *able* at this time in her life to trust you. It's not whether she *will* trust you or not, for that assumes that she is capable of trust at this moment. The question is whether she is *able* to trust you at this time. I think she is not able to trust. To trust another person is not something we can turn on or off simply by choosing to do so. Given the girl's background so far, she is strictly *unable* to trust another person.

Imagine further that you do not give up. You actively seek to be the girl's friend. You stand by her. Over a period of time you are consistently faithful to her. Even when she tests you by misbehaving, you do not give up on her. Finally, it happens that she does indeed come to trust you as a true friend. Coming to trust you is a major reorientation of her life. What made this reorientation possible was your reliable behavior. Your loyal, steadfast behavior *enabled* her to do what previously she was unable to do, namely, to trust you.

This example from a human relationship may help us understand what is involved in our relationship with God. To turn from trusting primarily in ourselves or some other creature to trusting in God is a fundamental reorientation of the self. Such a basic redirection is on a different level than choosing what clothes to wear, where to vacation, or what job to take. The Lutheran confessions say that when we trust primarily in ourselves or another creature, we are strictly unable to turn our lives over to God. Only God can bring about this reorientation. What enables us to trust above all else in God is God's own loving, faithful presence that *wins* our trust. Our trust is a response to God's loving presence. For Christians, this loving presence of God is seen most deeply in Jesus. As Paul says, "God proves his love for us in that while we still were sinners Christ died for us" (Romans 5:8). God's active love wins our trust and love. God enables us to do what previously we were unable to do.

Do we not feel conscious of giving our lives to the Lord? This may well be true. Some people have the experience of giving their allegiance to God. Is this not their choice? Let's return to our example of the distrustful eight-year-old girl whom you befriend. At some time in her relationship with you, she will be conscious of placing her trust in you. However, that moment comes very late in the process. What lays the groundwork for it are months, probably years, of reliable love on your part. What she experiences as her own choice of you as a faithful friend is a *response* to your faithfulness. If asked later about this, she would not stress the importance of her choice of you, but would emphasize your faithfulness that made her response possible. Similarly, in our relationship with God, we may be aware of giving our "selves" to God. It feels like a choice we have made and indeed it is. Yet that giving of self to God is a response wholly dependent on and made possible by God's faithfulness.

What is needed to set things right? This is a foundational question for orienting ourselves on our journey of life. Answering it involves an assessment of our own capabilities and an understanding of God. The first view sees humans as *slow*, the second as *weak*, and the third as *distrustful*. In other words, they differ in the level of readiness we have for communion with God. Are we simply slow learners? Are we weak yet basically willing folks who need help in establishing partnership with God? Or are we downright distrustful of God, and actually resist greater intimacy with our Creator? The three views also differ in their understanding of God. The first pictures God chiefly as *moral teacher,* the second sees God as *helper,* and the third regards the Lord mainly as *saving friend.*

The Lutheran confessions solidly maintain the third position. Actually there have been some variations within that stance, for example, between Martin Luther and Philip Melanchthon, and there have been Lutherans past and present who support the second position with its emphasis on a conversion experience and faith as a decision. So the Lutheran family has included some diversity, yet the core of the tradition represented by its confessional writings stands firm on seeing God as the saving friend who delivers us from our distrust and enables us to trust her.

CHARTING A COURSE

As wayfarers on the journey of life, we seek to chart a course. I have suggested that three questions are crucial to ask: What are we meant to be? What has gone wrong? What is needed to set things right? The Lutheran tradition of Christian faith answers these questions in the following way. First, we are meant to to be genuinely free persons whose hearts are devoted to God and caring toward other people and creatures. We are intended for close friendship with God, to love God, and to bask in being her beloved. When we enjoy this sort of relationship with God, we find freedom and peace within ourselves, and our hearts are open to other human beings and other creatures in God's world. Second, what has gone wrong is fundamentally that we are alienated from God, that we do not enjoy close friendship with our Creator. This state produces distortions within our selves and in our relationships with other people and creatures. Distortions become hardened features of social institutions and are passed on from generation to generation. Third, what is needed to set things right is for God to deliver us from the bondage of our own distrust and awaken love for her and others.

This is a simple vision for human life, yet it is by no means simplistic. The hard realities of the human condition are clearly acknowledged. What probably rubs most against the grain of widely accepted attitudes is the conviction that we are not able to reorient our lives, but are utterly dependent upon the goodness of God to deliver us from our own distrust and misdirected loving. We tend to be like addicts who claim over and over that they can quit their addiction on their own or with a little help. The Lutheran tradition says, though, that we are truly powerless to free ourselves. Only the grace of God can turn us around and bring us into that close friendship with God in which we trust and love him and enjoy his love.

FOR REFLECTION AND PRACTICE

1. Take fifteen minutes to reflect on the First Commandment and Luther's explanation of it in his Small Catechism. How do this commandment, its original context in which God reminds the Israelites that God is the one who has delivered them from bondage, and Luther's explanation of it connect with your life? (Note: *fear* in Luther's explanation does not mean *terror*, but rather deep respect and awe.)

> *You shall have no other gods.*

What does this mean?
Answer: We should fear, love, and trust in God above all things.[2]

What immediately precedes the First Commandment in Exodus 20:2-3 are these words of introduction to all the commandments, "I am the Lord your God, who brought you out of the land of Egypt, out of the house of slavery."

2. Slowly ponder a confession of sin frequently used at the beginning of a Lutheran worship service. This confession is often said quickly. Take ten minutes to look carefully at each part and ask to what extent these words can truly be your own. Printed below are the confession from the "Brief Order for Confession and Forgiveness" in the *Lutheran Book of Worship (LBW)* used by the Evangelical Lutheran Church in America and two options for confession in Divine Service I of *Lutheran Worship (LW)* used by The Lutheran Church—Missouri Synod.

Lutheran Book of Worship

> Most merciful God, we confess that we are in bondage to sin and cannot free ourselves. We have sinned against you in thought, word, and deed, by what we have done and by what we have left undone. We have not loved you with our whole heart; we have not loved our neighbors as ourselves. For the sake of your Son, Jesus Christ, have mercy on us. Forgive us, renew us, and lead us, so that we may delight in your will and walk in your ways, to the glory of your holy name. Amen.

Lutheran Worship

O almighty God, merciful Father, I, a poor, miserable sinner, confess to you all my sins and iniquities with which I have ever offended you and justly deserved your punishment now and forever. But I am heartily sorry for them and sincerely repent of them, and I pray you of your boundless mercy and for the sake of the holy, innocent, bitter sufferings and death of your beloved Son, Jesus Christ, to be gracious and merciful to me, a poor sinful being.

Or

Almighty God, our Maker and Redeemer, we poor sinners confess to you that we are by nature sinful and unclean and that we have sinned against you by thought, word, and deed; therefore we flee for refuge to your boundless mercy, seeking and imploring your grace for the sake of our Lord Jesus Christ.

If you are using these exercises in a group, first give each person time to complete the meditation alone before joining together. If the group is rather large, it would be better to share what happened in the meditation first in small clusters before coming together again as a total gathering.

3. Look over the three views presented in the section "What Is Needed to Set Things Right?" With which of these views do you agree. Why?

3

TRUST IN GOD'S
MERCIFUL GRACE

As we proceed on a spiritual journey, we inevitably form some view of our place in the larger scheme of things. Central to that view is an understanding of God, or Ultimate Reality, and our relationship with that Ultimate Reality. In our highly pluralistic age, we are confronted with many forms of spirituality, each of which promotes a certain relationship with God, or Ultimate Reality. For some types of New Age spirituality, a key element is guidance from other beings through channeling, which is supposed to help one advance to higher states of consciousness that bring one closer to God. Some forms of Goddess spirituality involve hilltop rituals at new moon as a vital way of connecting with deities closely associated with the rhythms of nature. For practicing Muslims, prayers at specific times of the day are part and parcel of devotion to God. Each form of spirituality involves a certain understanding of Ultimate Reality and encourages a specific kind of relationship with that reality. Indeed, the very core of a spirituality is the relationship with the transcendent that it fosters. So the most fundamental question to ask of any spirituality is this: What sort of relationship with God does it envision? And the most important question to ask oneself is: What is my relationship with God?

The very heart of Lutheran spirituality is that it seeks to foster a relationship of trust that God's merciful grace undergirds all of life. Stated in *doctrinal* terms, this is what Lutherans call justification by faith or, more accurately, justification by grace through faith. In the next section, we will have an opportunity to examine this doctrine, but first we will consider what it means to *live* justification by faith.

LIVING JUSTIFICATION BY FAITH

To live justification by faith is to have a certain kind of relationship with God. It's a relationship similar in some respects to that between you and a very close friend. Your friend knows you well, knows the significant events of your life, knows your good and bad points. But in addition to knowing you very well, your close friend also accepts you. Although aspects of your character are less than desirable and sometimes you act in hurtful ways, your friend forgives you. Another side of the relationship is that your friend will help you become a better person. Your friend will then encourage and help you do good, but will also challenge you when you hurt others. More and more, your friend and you will come to share certain values. You also do good things for your friend and present a gift from time to time. The reason you do these things is not to gain a friend. It's because you are already such good friends and care for one another that you do nice things and bring gifts.

Martin Luther thought the believer's relationship with God is similar. God knows us even better than our closest friend. The Lutheran tradition says faith in Jesus Christ brings two great treasures: assurance that God loves and accepts us, and the beginning of a life that is more Christlike. Assurance of God's love and acceptance is the bedrock of the relationship. Like a good friend, God also enables us to begin becoming a better person, which is to be more like Christ. God both inspires us to do good and, in love, critiques our shortcomings. While we will want to please God by doing good things and giving gifts, we do such things not in order to win God's goodwill. Rather, because we are on good terms with God, we do them willingly. The whole relationship is grounded in love and acceptance.

Of course, our relationship with God is not identical to a relationship with a human friend. After all, God is eternal, humans are mortal. God is holy and people are flawed. The qualities of our very best friend are just pale shadows of God's qualities. Thus the faith relationship with God is different in some respects from a friendship between two people. As creator, God gives us life and the world that sustains it. As reconciler, God reaches out to bring the separated together. As sanctifier, God begins to change our priorities immediately and promises eternal life in a renewed world. Paul's question to the Christians in Corinth applies to us all, "What do you have that you did not receive?" (1 Corinthians 4:7). To live with faith in God is fundamentally to trust that God loves us and wants to give us gift upon gift.

A biblical word for this quality of God is *grace*. The God about which Scripture speaks is a God of grace, a gift-giving or gracious God. The graciousness of God is manifested in many ways, but its central expression is Jesus Christ. Christians believe that in this human being God made friends with the world, "In Christ God was reconciling the world to himself" (2 Corinthians 5:19). When God's grace in Christ is accepted by faith, the Lutheran tradition says two major gifts are received. The most fundamental gift is God's mercy, which accepts us. Even though we sin and fall short in many ways, God forgives and accepts us. The other gift God gives at the same time is the transformation, the renewal, of our lives. Acceptance and renewal are the two central gifts that Christ brings. Since God's acceptance is always complete and renewal is always incomplete in this life, Lutherans stress that God's merciful acceptance is the bedrock on which our relationship with God is based. This understanding of grace in which renewal occurs, yet the primary accent falls on divine acceptance, is what I mean by God's *merciful grace*.

Another way to say all this is that the basic gift God gives is to be the eternal friend who loves, forgives, and sustains us in every situation. So what God gives first of all is not some *thing*, not even a "spiritual" something like "eternal life," but a *relationship* with God's own self. In this relationship we bask in God's loving acceptance and begin to become more like our friend.

The most fundamental element of Lutheran spirituality is to *live* in this relationship with God. So as the title of this book says, Lutheran spirituality is *A Graceful Life*, a life full of grace, grace that enables one to move through life with balance. This means to trust that God's merciful grace undergirds all of life. It is not automatic for us to live with trust in God. When things are going well for us, we are prone to trust primarily in ourselves or in what other people can do for us. We often find it even more difficult to trust in God when trouble comes, for it may seem as though God has abandoned us. So trusting in God does not come easily. Indeed, as we learn to trust more and more, we also discover that trusting itself is made possible by God. "What do you have that you did not receive?" All is gift. All is grace. "For by grace you have been saved through faith; and this is not your own doing, it is the gift of God" (Ephesians 2:8).

A Survey on Grace

To live with trust in God's merciful grace is foundational for Lutheran spirituality. Yet, as in complex human relationships, we have questions about what it means to live in this relationship with God. It helps to reflect further on the meaning of grace, faith, and good works. One way to do this is to respond to the following religious survey:

In thinking about one's Christian faith and daily life, *grace* can mean many different things to different people. Please read through the items listed below and check those that describe what grace means to you. (Check all that apply.)

1. For me *grace* means that God always cares for me no matter what I do.
2. For me *grace* means that God is always caring for me even when I feel abandoned by God.
3. For me *grace* means that God always cares for me, but I must try to live the best life I can.
4. For me *grace* means that God always cares for me, but I have to place my faith in God.
5. I don't think much about the concept of grace.
6. None of the above describes what *grace* means to me in my life and faith. To me *grace* means . . .[1]

It will benefit you the most if you mark your option or options before reading further.

Now let's look at the first four options. Option 1 says, "grace means that God always cares for me no matter what I do." Something very important is affirmed here, namely, the unconditional quality of God's love and acceptance. Since God's love has no strings attached, no fine print that restricts it, we can be assured that God welcomes everyone no matter who they are or what they have done. God loves the liar, the thief, and even the abuser, rapist, and murderer. This does not mean that God approves of what they have done. In fact, the Bible frequently speaks of God's opposition and wrath toward injustice. Nevertheless, God does not cease to care for those who do wrong.

It may help to compare this to the human relationship of parent and child. Parents often continue to love their son or daughter no matter what the child has done. Parents of a murderer grieve over the crime, but they usually still love their offspring. Does this mean that they don't care if their son or daughter kills again? Not at all. Their love wants what is best for their son or daughter, and committing another murder is bad both for the victim and the killer. It is similar with God's love. God always cares for us and seeks what is best for us. Such unconditional love is not a license to do whatever evil might enter our mind, but is an invitation to respond to God with love. God's unconditional love is the foundation of a friendship relation with God. So whether option 1 is sound depends on one's interpretation of "God always cares for me no matter what I do."

Option 2 says, "grace means that God is always caring for me even when I feel abandoned by God." This is a statement that we can endorse without qualification. At times we do not feel lovable. Depression is a frightful reality for many of us. When we're depressed, we don't feel loved or lovable. At other times, we may experience a tragic loss. It seems to us as though the roof has caved in. We may feel as though God is aloof and uncaring. In such situations the message of God's grace is extra good news, although it may take some time for that news to reach home. In the relationship of grace, God loves us even when we do not feel that we are loved.

Option 3 says, "grace means that God always cares for me but I must try to live the best life I can." This raises what is often called the issue of good works. To be sure, those who believe in Jesus Christ should try to live the best life they can, but a critical question about good works is the *motive* for doing them. The Lutheran confessional writings emphasize that genuine good works are done out of love. This is not romantic love, but love in the sense of seeking what is best for someone. Furthermore, this love is most pure when it is willing, rather than done with a grudging spirit or ulterior motive. In other words, it is important not only to do what will help someone but also to do it willingly. For example, when people are starving, to give money to feed them is doing what is good for the starving people. But the reason a person contributes this money might be that, as a prominent public figure, he or she has an image to maintain. In that case, the person's motive is not gladly to help the starving, but is selfish and influenced by social duress.

This point about motive is relevant to our relationship with God. Not many people think they can actually earn God's goodwill on their own; nearly all of us realize that we all have some faults and need God's indulgence. But it is quite common to think of our relationship with God as rather like a business relationship in which God does one part, but we must do our part as well. Even though God's part may be thought of as greater than ours, it is still like a business deal. In that case, trying to live the best life we can is like living up to our part of a bargain. Bargaining is hardly the spirit that pervades a relationship between two people who love each other. When two people love each other, they do things for one another willingly and without thought for what each gets in return. So in relationship with God, the question of spirit or motive is the key to trying to "live the best life I can."

Option 4 says, "grace means that God always cares for me, but I have to place my faith in God." There is something right about this statement. Since we have a personal relationship with God, there is a certain mutuality about it. Faith in God is vital for us to be involved in the relationship. But so much depends on how we think of the faith relationship with God, for again it's possible to think of this relationship like a business exchange, only now the stress is on our act of faith. To think of it this way misses the active quality of God's love. Once more it may be helpful to think of a parent-child relation. Imagine that a parent and child have become estranged, but that the parent loves the child and is willing to forgive past hurts. Reconciliation will not occur until the child accepts that love and forgiveness. Similarly, faith in God's grace is necessary. However, like a good parent, God does not merely wait passively for us to respond in faith. God seeks us out and, by telling us of the divine love and forgiveness, seeks to evoke the response of faith in us. God actively works to *win* our trust.

So what is the right answer to the survey inquiry about the meaning of grace? Each of the first four answers voices a legitimate concern, but several also have limitations. This is a testimony to the simple yet complex nature of the grace-filled relationship with God. This simplicity with complexity should not surprise us, for we encounter it also in our deep relationships with one another. On one level, the relationship between two intimate friends is simple and natural, like breathing. Yet we also know from experience that a long-term friendship is also difficult both to live and to understand. Living as close friends day after day, year after year, involves all sorts of ups and downs. And when we step back and ask questions about the nature of true friendship, we discover complexities that resist simplistic formulation. If this is true of our purely human relationships, how much more must it be the case in our relationship with God? So in some respects a grace-filled relationship with God is as easy and simple as unlabored breathing, but in other ways it is difficult and complicated. No matter where we are in our own relationship with God, it is always possible to go deeper both in the relationship and in our understanding of it.

Going Deeper

Actually living with trust in God's merciful grace in Christ is what matters most. But in order to foster that way of living, Lutherans have emphasized the doctrine of justification by grace through faith. In this section, we will examine this doctrine of justification more closely. While it is entirely possible to trust in God's merciful grace without understanding the finer points of the doctrine of justification, the doctrine may deepen both one's understanding and appreciation of God's grace.

In speaking of salvation, the apostle Paul says it is by grace alone that people are justified—that is, become right with God. Paul frequently contrasts grace with receiving what one merits. In relation to

God we all are sinners. So Paul says, "For there is no distinction, since all have sinned and fall short of the glory of God; they are now justified by his grace as a gift, through the redemption that is in Christ Jesus" (Romans 3:23-24). Paul says that we are justified, or put right, only by God's grace.

However, this does not settle everything, for there are two aspects of this redemptive grace. Some church traditions place the primary emphasis on one aspect of grace, while other church traditions put the accent on the other form of grace.

TRANSFORMING GRACE

One aspect of God's gracious activity is to transform people by making them more faithful, loving, and righteous. This understanding of grace was emphasized by the influential theologian St. Augustine (354–430). Augustine held that while all of us have many values, the key to our lives is what we value most. In other words, the central question is, What are our priorities? What do we love most of all? According to Augustine, the essential fault within human beings is that they love some creature more than God. What they love most may be themselves, their family, money, or prestige, but it is still a creature. According to Augustine, these things can never bring true happiness and contentment; he believed that the human heart can find true satisfaction and peace only if its first love is God. As we saw in the previous chapter, this understanding of the human situation is shared by the Lutheran confessions.

The primary work of God's grace, according to Augustine, is to reorder a person's priorities so that the person comes to love God above all else. Thus divine grace is primarily a process that transforms a person by changing his or her priorities, thereby making the person more faithful, loving, and righteous. This understanding of grace has been dominant in the Roman Catholic tradition and finds similar expression in the Eastern Orthodox concept of salvation as participation in the life of God.

What Martin Luther encountered as a young monk and scholar was an altered understanding of transforming grace. Whereas Augustine had said that salvation comes by God's grace alone, most later medieval theology said that salvation comes through a combination of God's grace and human effort. Sometimes it is said that Roman Catholicism taught salvation through good works, while Lutheranism taught salvation by grace. This conviction is too crude. Rather, Catholic theology of Luther's era commonly held that both God and the human being contributed something to salvation.

Martin Luther experienced intense personal unrest with this understanding of God's transforming grace. He worried whether his contribution to salvation had been enough. His unrest led him to question Augustine's whole approach of making God's transforming grace the primary factor in salvation, for that approach would not let Luther have assurance that he was in right relation with God. The problem for Luther was this: In this life, God's grace only partially transforms a person. The process is never complete; prior to death, one never perfectly loves God above all things. Sin continues to cling to a person until one is finally raised from the dead and made totally holy. So Luther wondered, How can I be sure that God accepts me? This was the question that burned in Luther's heart.

Accepting Grace

Through persistent meditation on Scripture and especially Paul's Epistle to the Romans, Luther found his answer in the other aspect of God's gracious activity—accepting grace or God's favor. Perhaps the most memorable biblical testimony to divine forgiveness is the parable of the prodigal son (Luke 15:11-32). In the story, a rich man's younger son takes his inheritance to a distant country and wastes it on "immoral" living. Finally, when he is destitute and miserable, he decides to return home and admit his wrongdoing to his father. Before the son even arrives at the house, his father comes out to meet him and welcomes him back with great joy and affection. Indeed, much to the displeasure of the always-dutiful older son, the father seems to ignore the dictates of justice by accepting the wayward son without penalty or reservation. The parable communicates God's kind generosity in simply forgiving sin. Remembering this form of divine grace gave Martin Luther peace, for even though he would be plagued with sin until death, the gospel of Jesus Christ assured him that God forgives the sins of those who trust in Jesus.

For Christians, it is not a question of choosing *either* God's transforming grace *or* God's accepting grace, for all Christian traditions recognize both aspects of divine grace. This is also true of Martin Luther, who called attention to the two forms of grace by frequently distinguishing between two corresponding forms of righteousness. *Righteousness* is not a word that we use much in everyday speech, but it is an important word in the New Testament, where *righteous* and *justification* are two forms of the Greek word *dikaio*. In order to be justified, or in the right, before God, one must be righteous. What Luther emphasized is that there are two kinds of righteousness that correspond to the two forms of God's grace. On the one hand, there is the grace of God that transforms people so that their priorities are changed and they are made righteous and able to more nearly conform to God's will. On the other hand, there is the grace of God that forgives people; it is as though they have appeared before God in court and have been pronounced righteous. Thus there is a distinction between grace that transforms or *makes righteous*, and grace that accepts or *declares righteous*.

This distinction helps us better understand Luther's teaching of justification by grace through faith. The gospel of Jesus Christ announces that we are justified by grace through faith. Let's analyze each part of this statement.

1. We are *justified by grace*. *Grace* here includes both meanings of grace—the grace that declares one righteous and the grace that makes one righteous. Both divine gifts are effective in justification. But whereas Roman Catholic and Orthodox teaching regard transforming grace as primary, for Luther being forgiven or declared righteous is the *primary* form of grace, primary in the sense of being the ground of assurance that one is accepted by God. At the same time, says Luther, God's grace is also at work transforming a person by making him or her more righteous, faithful, and holy. In fact, faith itself is a sign that God's grace is already at work, for faith rests secure in God's forgiving grace and the very act of faith itself is a result of God's transforming grace in a person's life.[2] But since this transformative work of

grace is always partial and incomplete during this life on earth, Luther stresses that the solid ground of confidence before God is God's acceptance or forgiveness of sin. This primary emphasis on forgiveness is suggested by my formulation of the principle of Lutheran spirituality as trust in the *merciful* grace of God.

Later Protestant theologians commonly used the term *justification* in a more limited sense as the forgiving grace that declares righteous, and then employed the term *sanctification* to designate the transforming grace that makes righteous. This practice was followed by the Lutheran Formula of Concord (1577) and most later Lutheran theologians.[3] A benefit of this distinction between justification and sanctification was to make clear that the sole ground of peace with the Creator is God's merciful acceptance, not in any way our holiness. A negative effect of the distinction was the tendency to separate the two aspects of God's gracious activity.

In other words, the Lutheran tradition has used *justification* in two senses. *Justification* in the broad sense includes both the accepting and transforming grace of God. *Justification* in the narrow sense refers only to God's accepting grace, while *sanctification* points to transforming grace. In our discussion, I use *justification* in the broad sense, unless otherwise specified. An advantage of following this broad usage is that it makes it easier to see the connections of Lutheran teaching with other traditions, such as Roman Catholic and Orthodox.

2. The second part of Luther's teaching of justification is that we are justified *through faith*. This is not just any faith such as faith in oneself or in one's nation. According to Luther, we are justified through faith in Jesus Christ. Faith includes belief, in this case, some beliefs about Jesus Christ. But the core of faith for Luther is trust. Luther envisions trust as clinging to Christ much like a drowning person clings to his or her rescuer.

The fundamental point is this: What God wants to happen is a new relationship of a person with God. This new relationship is created when a person has faith in Jesus Christ, for then he or she relies upon Christ and commits all of life to him. One of Luther's favorite images for this new relationship of faith in Christ is the biblical image of a bride united with her bridegroom (Ephesians 5:31-32). Luther says that in this marriage, there is a happy exchange. That is, Christ claims as his own the believer's sin and mortality, and gives to the believer his holiness and life. So Jesus' combat with sin and death not only happened long ago in Palestine but happens now also in the life of the believer. The believer is now seen as perfectly holy in God's eyes (forgiveness) and begins to manifest goodness and justice in his or her words and actions (transformation). However, all this occurs only within the intimate relationship of faith in Christ. If a person were to break the marriage bond with Christ and try to go it alone, then he or she would again be trapped within sin and mortality.[4]

Now we can better understand the relation between faith and good works. According to Martin Luther, the primary source of good deeds is Jesus Christ living and present within the believer. Faith is not merely believing that Jesus died for our sins long ago. Faith is trust in the present Christ, loving him, seeking from him all that is best. This notion of Christ present is often hard to grasp. A great many Christians think of Jesus mainly as someone who long ago set an example and paid the price for their sins. In such an understanding, Christ accomplished mighty things in the past and now dwells in heaven. Such a Christ feels rather distant. But for Luther, Jesus Christ is alive and very much present in and with the believer. Luther had a powerful sense of living day by day in the intimate companionship of Jesus. To be sure, there were times in Luther's life when Jesus seemed far off, and these were periods of struggle and anguish for him. In those periods, he looked for ways to remind himself that Christ was really present with him. Luther's understanding of faith as devotion to the present Christ has been pivotal for many Lutherans.

The stronger this relationship of friendship and devotion to Jesus Christ, the more the believer gladly acts out of love. This is how faith is active in love. What is meant by faith is not merely holding certain beliefs, but an intimate relationship with Jesus Christ marked by trust and devotion. Sometimes it is said that good works come from gratitude for what God has done. Gratitude is surely a factor in this relationship, but it is not the most basic. Gratitude is our subjective attitude. More basic is the foundation of our gratitude, and that foundation is Christ, the present Christ. The present Christ is the primary source of the believer's good works, for in a relationship of intimate friendship and devotion to this Christ, one's values and attitudes become more like Christ's.

GETTING DOWN TO CASES

Thinking about God's grace in Christ is rather complex conceptually, but when it comes to actually living with trust in that grace, we encounter difficulties of another kind. What does it mean to trust that God's grace always undergirds life? Several specific cases will help us wrestle with the question.

Case 1: Pastor Anderson has a solid understanding of the Lutheran teaching of justification by grace through faith. He got a thorough drilling on the subject already in his own confirmation instruction, and seminary training deepened his grasp of the topic. So when he leads his confirmation class in a unit on the Lutheran Reformation, he knows what he is talking about. He makes it very clear that we are saved by God's grace, not by our good works. He always feels good about doing such a competent job with that important topic. What Pastor Anderson does not feel good about, though, is how the long hours he puts in on church work don't leave him much time for his family. He takes time here and there to be with his wife and kids, but those times are often sacrificed to work. He and his wife have talked about this, for he wants to be a good husband and father. It is not that the church council is pressuring him to work so hard. But Pastor Anderson feels something inside himself constantly pushing him. He feels good about himself when he does a task well. It gives him a sense of value and worth. But the feeling lasts only a short time, and then he needs to undertake another task. Sometimes he feels like he's on an endless treadmill, and he gets depressed.

Commentary: It appears that Pastor Anderson is a workaholic. What drives his addiction to work is his quest for personal worth through successful completion of tasks. Yet he can never find peace and rest in this, for he must keep on establishing his value through ever new accomplishments.

Although Pastor Anderson knows the doctrine of justification by grace in his head and has applied it to certain aspects of his life, it has not penetrated to some of the deeper levels of his heart and daily life. He understands that he cannot win his way to heaven by good deeds. But isn't his effort to establish personal worth through his accomplishments a subtle form of self-justification? Isn't he trying to affirm his own goodness and righteousness by his success at work? Pastor Anderson probably would deny that he is attempting to justify himself before God. But shouldn't God's opinion of us be the factor that most influences our perceptions of ourselves? When we believe in our heart that God loves and values us, that belief gives us a powerful sense of worth. When justification by grace penetrates the heart, we feel worthwhile and are set free from the burdensome quest to establish our own value.

As we have noted several times, the doctrine of justification by grace through faith is an abstract way of talking about a relationship of trust in a loving, merciful God who intends to make us like Jesus. On the one hand, it is possible for someone to have that relationship with God without being able to articulate the doctrine of justification by grace. On the other hand, Pastor Anderson demonstrates that it is also possible to know the intricacies of the doctrine of justification even while trust in God's merciful love has not yet reached some aspects of one's life.

Case 2: Sara is very angry. She is thirty-eight years old and the single mother of two young children. She has struggled through many trials. Her divorce was difficult, to say the least. Not only did it give her deep feelings of failure and loss that made her depressed, but she also had the sole responsibility of managing the details of family life and finances. It took her a while, but she came through the hard times stronger than ever. She had started feeling good about herself and good about her kids. In the whole difficult process, her faith in the Lord had grown. Having bedtime prayers with the kids had become a special time of closeness with one another and with God. But then she got sick. During her regular monthly self-examination, she felt a lump in her left breast. When she went to the doctor and tests were done, it was determined that she had cancer. The lab report after surgery revealed that the cancer had spread into four lymph nodes, so she began chemotherapy and radiation treatments. She handled the treatments amazingly well, but now she is worried about her kids—only six and nine years old. What if the cancer returns and she dies? What would become of the kids? She's as angry as can be. She's angry with her body for letting her down. She's angry with God for letting this happen. It's so unfair. Sara knows that she hasn't been perfect. But she had asked forgiveness for her sins, and her relationship with God had recently revived and deepened. Life was just getting good and now this. It's so unfair.

Commentary: One might wonder whether justification by grace through faith has any relevance to Sara's situation, for she has received forgiveness of her sins and is not worried whether God will accept her into heaven. Her concerns are about living longer and the future of her kids. What does justification have to do with that? Much depends on the meaning of justification. If one follows later Lutheran practice and limits justification to God's forgiveness, then it seems more peripheral to her situation. But if we follow Luther's frequent practice of including both aspects of grace under justification, then it is relevant.

In Luther's understanding, to live as a justified son or daughter of God is to live with trust that God's grace undergirds *all* aspects of life. In his masterful treatise "The Freedom of a Christian," Luther says Christian freedom is not only deliverance from petty religious obligations or trusting in good works but also power over suffering and death. "The power of which we speak is spiritual. It rules in the midst of enemies and is powerful in the midst of oppression. This means nothing else than that 'power is made perfect in weakness' [2 Corinthians 12:9] and that in all things I can find profit toward salvation [Romans 8:28], so that the cross and death itself are compelled to serve me and to work together with me for my salvation. This is a splendid privilege and hard to attain. . . ."[5] The freedom of which Luther speaks in this treatise is both freedom from uncertainty of how we stand with God through accepting grace and freedom from domination by sin and death through transforming grace. The latter freedom is especially pertinent to Sara's situation, for her life and the security of her children are threatened.

To have faith in God's grace is to trust that God loves us and always seeks what is best for us. What is best for us is closely linked with Jesus. Not a dead Jesus who merely lived long ago, but a living Jesus who is present right now. To believe in God's grace is to trust that God wants what is best for us in Christ.

The hard truth, however, is that when our lives are falling apart, often we are not able to see how a loving God is seeking what is best for us. That is the case with Sara who feels her life threatened by cancer and worries about the future of her two children. She wonders, How could a loving God let such a thing happen? It's not surprising that Sara is angry. Many people have proposed answers to the question of how a loving God can let evil occur, but probably there is no answer that will satisfy Sara at this time. Scripture does not give neat theoretical answers to suffering, but it offers a different sort of assurance.

First, Scripture lets Sara know she is not the first to feel puzzlement or anger in the midst of trouble. One psalmist scolds God, "Rouse yourself! Why do you sleep, O Lord?" (Psalm 44:23). Another feels abandoned by God: "My God, my God, why have you forsaken me?" (Psalm 22:1), and Jesus cries these same words from the cross (Mark 15:34). Thus it is all right to express doubt, frustration, and anger to God.

Second, Scripture gives us some indication of how God works. Naturally, we want God to remove suffering. Sometimes that happens, but other times it does not. In the Garden of Gethsemane the night before his crucifixion, Jesus prayed, "Remove this cup from me" (Mark 14:36). That did not happen. Jesus had to go through the suffering rather than around it. Why does God not quickly deliver us from suffering? The fact that God did not spare Jesus from the cross tells us something very significant about the way God works. It is not God's highest goal to have each of us live a long, carefree life. God is more interested in fashioning people who have deep faith in God and love for one another. Those are the primary characteristics of Jesus, and it is God's goal to conform us to Christ. According to Christian beliefs, this goal is ultimately what is best for us. We may still have lots of unanswered questions. Why *this* suffering? Why *now*? In this life we'll probably never be able to find satisfying answers to all our questions.

Third and most important is the assurance that God understands and shares our suffering. If God were just a spectator to suffering, we would have good reason to accuse the Lord of cold cruelty. But God's unique presence in Jesus tells us that God is not a cool bystander to our pain; God entered into the very depths of human tribulation. The mother of a seriously ill child feels the child's misery as her own; she is anxious, distressed, and sleeps poorly. In similar fashion, God's special presence in the suffering Jesus assures us that our Creator shares our plight.

To live as a justified son or daughter of God is to trust that God's gracious love undergirds everything in life. This does not mean one must believe that God causes everything to happen; for example, that God directly caused Sara's cancer. So often we cannot see any purpose in something bad. Yet there is the opportunity to believe that somehow God's love is at work in and through those bad things.

I myself have some experience of this. When I got colon cancer, I cried a lot over the threat to my life. I had so much to live for—above all, my wife and children. But over time, facing the prospect of death has allowed God to give me a calm and peace about death, which is a very precious gift of love. In and through the evil of cancer, God has deepened my faith and enabled me to reach out in new ways to other people. Along with the serenity of knowing that God fully accepted me came—gradually, through transforming grace—a more fragile contentment with the possibility of giving up my wife and children.

Case 3: Mark, a twenty-three-year-old African American, is now seriously considering the Christian church. As a teenager he had stayed aloof, although his mother and father were devout Christians. He had felt that Christianity was the white man's religion, and he knew the Bible had been used to justify slavery and white supremacy. His parents told him that blacks had made Christianity their own, but he hadn't been convinced. Now that he will be getting married soon, he's been thinking more seriously about his life and future. His fiancée is a Christian and takes her faith seriously, so Mark is considering his own faith more deeply. He has been attending a class held by the pastor of his parents' Lutheran church.

The pastor, an African American, talked about justification by grace through faith. The pastor said *justification by grace* means two things. One is that you are somebody, you are valuable, since God loves and accepts you. Everyone comes before God as a poor sinner; differences in color, economic status, and social position count for nothing. When you believe that in mercy God forgives and accepts you, then you are somebody. The other meaning of *justification* is that it involves justice not only before God, but also with other people. The pastor said *justification by grace* means a changed life in which a person helps those who are oppressed and seeks reconciliation across social barriers.

Commentary: Whenever we interpret something from the Bible, a conversation takes place between the words of Scripture and ourselves in our life situation. We bring to Scripture our distinctive life experience and needs, which color what we see and hear in the text. For example, Sara, the young mother with breast cancer, is now likely to see elements of meaning in Psalm 23 that she had previously overlooked. The experience of racial and economic inequality creates an interpretation of Scripture that is likely hidden from most white middle-class Lutherans because they belong to the dominant group. But race and class are significant, self-conscious factors in the interpretation of justification given by the pastor.

As a black in America, Mark grew up in a society with messages telling him that he is inferior. In this context, the message of justification by grace through faith affirms that Mark is a valuable person loved by God. This affirmation is the impact of the loving, accepting grace of God. The African American pastor also continues on to emphasize the transforming grace of God that leads a person to care about others and to work for greater justice in society. In this respect also, Mark's position in society affects his understanding of the relevance of justification for social justice.[6]

The primary thrust of God's accepting grace differs according to a person's need. What many people need most acutely is God's forgiveness of personal sin. But what some others need most at this point in life is God's affirmation of their value when they do not feel valuable. Not only is this need the case in Mark's situation, but it's also true with women who have experienced physical or sexual abuse. What a rape victim needs most after the trauma is not forgiveness for any sin of her own, but rather the assurance that God loves and values her.[7] To be sure, everyone stands in need of divine forgiveness, for none of us has clean hands. Yet the main thrust of God's acceptance varies with our situation.

The message of justification by grace is balm for all who experience a depleted self. As we noted in the previous chapter, many people live to various degrees with a depleted self, for they feel insignificant and empty. Sometimes this is because one has internalized negative messages about one's race, gender, or economic status. It can come when a period of success is followed by questioning whether success is all there is. The depleted self can also come when a time of sampling various religions, spiritualities, or philosophies ends with deep questions about whether there is any grand meaning to human existence. When we experience the depleted self, what we need most of all is the confidence and love of another. The trust and care of a human other is important, but the message of justification by grace goes beyond that to offer the confidence and love of God.

I recall talking with a professional woman in her mid-fifties, a mother of several children. A few years earlier, she had been a high school dropout married to an abusive, alcoholic husband. With tearful gratitude, this woman told that when she had expressed a desire for a college education, her pastor affirmed her desire and urged her to start with getting a high school equivalency degree. She said, "No one ever believed in me before." Now she has both a bachelor's and a master's degree. She found another human being who had confidence in her.

The message of justification by grace through faith goes deeper, for it tells us that in God's eyes we are always valuable, always loved, always accepted. God is the eternal Other whose affirmation and strength never leave us. Human affirmation is very significant, but what undergirds that and exists even where human affirmation fails is God's affirmation of us in Christ. "For the Son of God, Jesus Christ . . . was not 'Yes and No'; but in him it is always 'Yes.' For in him every one of God's promises is a 'Yes'" (2 Corinthians 1:19-20).

Case 4: Sometimes Christine wonders whether she is really a Christian, because she doesn't feel the way it seems she ought to. From her experience of growing up in the Lutheran church, she's heard the message that she's supposed to feel very sorry for her sins and then be joyful when she remembers the message of God's forgiveness in Christ. On Sundays the liturgy always begins with a somber confession of sins and the announcement of forgiveness. The heart of Holy Communion appears to be the same thing all over again. Then, somehow she's gotten the impression that her bedtime prayers are also meant to include serious requests for forgiveness. It's as though she is supposed to ride an emotional roller coaster going from the depths of sorrow to the peaks of happiness. But Christine's own relationship with God does not follow that roller coaster. Oh, sure, she has felt bad about something she has done, and been very glad to remember that God is forgiving. But most of the time she goes along with the quiet confidence that God loves her and accepts her as she is. To Christine, God is like an understanding, compassionate friend who fully accepts her. It is wonderful to have that quiet assurance. But she wonders whether she has got it right. Is she a real Christian?

Commentary: Martin Luther's own religious experience was marked by sharp contrasts. Like every other Christian, Luther's religious experience was shaped not only by the Bible but also by his culture and the church life of his day. In his biography of Luther, James Kittelson says the religion of Luther's early years was a search for spiritual security in which pilgrimages, saints, relics, images of death, and pictures of divine judgment were prominent.[8] It is not surprising that in this context Luther often felt terror at the awful wrath of God toward sin and experienced Satan as a real evil power pulling him down. In this situation, he also knew immense peace and joy in attending to the gospel that, in Christ, God is merciful and loving. So Luther's spiritual life did go through strong oscillations. But not every Christian will follow this pattern of experience. Christine's experience of God's grace is just as legitimate as Luther's. After all, what counts is not the nature of our religious experience, whether it be dramatic or ordinary, steady or oscillating, whether we've had a sudden conversion experience of being born again or have gradually grown in faith. What matters is our relationship with Christ. Since we are different people living in different situations, the particulars of our relationship with Christ will also vary. We do not need to conform to one pattern.

The four cases considered in this section are indicative of substantial diversity in the understanding and meaning of the Lutheran doctrine of justification by grace through faith. This should not surprise us, since we are basically reflecting on the grace-filled relationship with God. While God is constant, the impact of God's grace on the life of individuals and groups varies with different situations.

A FAMILY CONVERSATION

Diversity in the understanding and experience of justification for people today and in the history of Lutheranism is one reason for speaking of the Lutheran family of spirituality. Members of a family are not clones, but they bear some resemblance to one another. One common feature of Lutheran spirituality is living justification by grace through faith. Yet when we look closer, we see some diversity in the understanding of justification among Lutherans. So what unifies Lutherans? What makes them one family? I suggest that the main source of unity in this family is informed conversation with Scripture and the Lutheran confessions.

An analogy will explain what I mean. Recently I went to a quilt show at which my wife had volunteered to work. Since her shift had not yet ended, I began to look at the quilts. Some patterns caught my eye; others did not. When Marion's replacement arrived, she joined me in looking at the quilts. I said, "This quilt has a good way of expressing the bonds of love in marriage with interlocking rings of colored cloth." Marion said, "Yes, but it would be even better if she had quilted the white patches inside the colored rings." I looked again. Sure enough. The patches of white cloth inside the colored rings were just plain white cloth without any stitching on them. On another quilt nearby I noticed how another artist had adorned white background pieces with intricate stitching. As we continued, my wife pointed out other features of the art of quilting that had previously escaped me: the difference between machine and hand stitching, how expert hand stitching has tiny, even stitches, that some quilts were made up of a great many small pieces of material all sewn together.

When my wife was called away for a while, I stood close to the quilt that had been awarded first prize in the show and I listened to what people said about it. Some merely glanced at the quilt before quickly moving on; apparently they had just wandered into the show because of its proximity to other exhibits and had no understanding or appreciation of the craft. Two experienced quilters examined the quilt for a long time, and discussed in detail several of its fine points. Another woman was so touched at seeing a certain feature in the quilt's pattern that several tears ran down her face; to her husband she said her mother had incorporated that same feature into many of her quilts. When Marion returned, she said that all the judges had ranked this quilt very high, but it had not been the unanimous first choice.

I suggest that the ways people interpret a quilt (film, book, or antique cars, etc.) are like the ways people interpret justification by grace through faith. Because there are widely differing opinions offered about the prize quilt, one might cynically conclude that nobody really knows, that one opinion is just as good as another. But only someone ignorant of quilting thinks that. The more one learns about the art of quilting, the more one is able to make informed distinctions among quilts. The same is true of the Lutheran understanding of God's grace in Christ. The more one grows in understanding of grace in Scripture, Lutheran tradition, and other Christian traditions, the more one is able to make informed evaluations of different interpretations put forward. Nevertheless, there is not just one authentic view possible. Even distinguished experts may disagree on fine points. The quilt show judges were all highly qualified, yet they did not entirely agree. Similarly, scholars and theologians may have extensive knowledge of Scripture, Luther's theology, and the Lutheran confessions, yet they may disagree on certain matters.

One source of difference lies in the life experiences of the interpreter. As we noted, one woman was deeply touched by a particular feature in the prize-winning quilt because it brought back memories of her mother. To her that specific feature was the most significant element of the whole quilt. Likewise in the history of Lutheranism, Martin Luther's experiences were different from John Arndt's, and both are different from the experiences of contemporary Lutherans in Sweden or Tanzania or the United States. Another source of difference is that there are often different "schools" within a given field. Each school values certain qualities more highly than others. As there are various schools or approaches to quilting, so there are different schools of thought in Lutheran theology. Lutheran orthodoxy and pietism are two historic schools of thought, but there are others.

As we look back over this chapter, we can see that we have focused attention on two kinds of relationship. Most basic is the relationship with God that is spoken about in the doctrine of justification by grace through faith. I have said the essence of justification is to trust that God's grace in Christ undergirds all of life. This grace found in relationship with the living Christ includes both full acceptance from God and the beginnings of a transformed life with God-centered priorities. In addition, we have talked briefly about the relationships that Lutheran Christians have with one another, for Lutherans sometimes have disagreed among themselves about the precise understanding of justification. While some interpretations should be rejected as not well-informed in Scripture and Lutheran tradition, I have suggested that Lutherans should accept a range of legitimate views in the family conversation.

For Reflection and Practice

1. *Meditation on grace in one's own life.* Set aside ten to fifteen minutes in which you are not likely to be interrupted. Sit quietly in a comfortable position and close your eyes. Begin your meditative prayer by asking God's blessing on this meditation. Now recall any signs of God's grace in your life during a certain time period; it can be your lifetime or the past year, month, week, or day. There is no need to rush or to remember every event; just unhurriedly savor the manifestations of grace that come to mind. When you are finished or the time is up, give thanks to God for the signs of grace remembered. If you are doing this with others, insofar as you are comfortable, you may share your thoughts with two or three others.

2. *Imaginative meditation of Scripture.* Set aside ten to fifteen minutes of quiet time for this meditation, and sit in a comfortable position. One of the basic forms of meditation with Scripture is to imagine yourself as a participant in a biblical story. Quickly read through Luke 15:3-10 and select one of the two parables for your meditation. Then read that parable again, perhaps several times. If you choose verses 3-7, imagine yourself as the lost sheep. How have you become lost? How does it feel to be lost? How has the shepherd found you? What are your feelings about the shepherd? If you pick verses 8-10 for your meditation, imagine yourself as the lost coin. How have you become lost? How does it feel? What are your feelings about the woman who has found you? If you are doing this in a group, when you are done with the meditation you may share whatever thoughts you wish with several others in a subgroup before a whole group discussion.

3. *Meditation on a poem of thanks.* When a person lives with trust that God's grace in Christ undergirds all of life, then one has gratitude to God. As trust in God's redemptive grace deepens, one becomes more attuned to manifestations of God's generous love throughout all areas of life. God's generous love is perceived not only in forgiveness and Christian faith but also in the gift of life, nature, human bonds of love, and somehow paradoxically in the dark side of existence. Thankfulness deepens and broadens. The following poem by Lilly Gracia Christensen is a fine

expression of gratitude to God in all facets of life; it is powerful testimony
to a life full of grace. Read through the poem slowly, taking time to pause
and dwell on any phrase that especially speaks to you. It's all right if you
spend the entire time on just one part. The main purpose is to commune
with God in prayer, not necessarily to cover the whole poem.

I Would Give Thanks

for the sheer wonder of life,
　　dipped day upon day from
　　eternal springs, and held to
　　the thirsting lips of all
　　creatures;

for the beauty of God's wide world,
　　the fragrance of rain and the
　　lilt of wind, the marvel of
　　clouds and mountains and seas;

for the simple grace of laughter,
　　silver-clear above sounds
　　of strife;

for the challenge of new
　　beginnings, of goals attained
　　and vistas opening, of
　　failures forgiven and hope
　　new-sprung;

for the unspeakable privilege of
　　working with God, bearing
　　together a fragment of the
　　world's dread burden of sin,
　　drinking together a little of
　　the lonely bitter cup,
　　rejoicing together, too, with
　　Him in a foretaste of another
　　joy;

for the high vision of earth's
　　great souls, whom neither
　　sword nor fire nor want nor
　　hate could swerve from running
　　the race, nor from straining
　　toward the beckoning goal;

for the sacredness of human
　　suffering, for the ministry of
　　sorrow and pain, leading us

close to the heart of God,
　　slipping our hands like
　　children's into the almighty
　　hand;

for the reality of love,
　　rooted in God, flowing in
　　perfect freedom, blasting all
　　barriers and welding humanity
　　into the kinship of spirit;

for the terrible patience of God,
　　loving to the uttermost,
　　pouring out the most
　　precious of oblations on the
　　cold, unresponsive altar of
　　the unrepentant heart;

for the undimmed power of the
　　cross, planted deep in the
　　heart of the universe, eternal
　　embodiment and revelation of
　　the divine love;

for the changelessness of God,
　　from day to day and from age
　　to age the same, unmovable
　　rock, tender shepherd of
　　souls, source of perfect peace
　　and freedom, fount of life and
　　fathomless love;

and for the gift of a grateful
　　heart, sharing in the building
　　of a timeless temple, a temple
　　not made with hands—a temple
　　of praise which God eternally
　　inhabits.[9]

4. *Meditation on liturgical absolution.* Following the confession of sins at the beginning of the common Sunday liturgy, Lutherans are accustomed to hearing an absolution pronounced by a minister. Set aside five to ten minutes to listen closely to what is said in that absolution. Slowly read through the absolution(s) customarily used in your church and ponder the meaning of each phrase for you. Printed below are the two absolutions given as options in Divine Service I of *Lutheran Worship* used by The Lutheran Church—Missouri Synod and the *Lutheran Book of Worship* used by the Evangelical Lutheran Church in America. You may note that in both cases the first absolution speaks in specific terms only of the grace of forgiveness, while the second absolution speaks also of transforming grace. If you do this as part of a group, break into small groups of three or four and share your meditations with one another. Discussion among the whole group may follow.

Lutheran Worship

Upon this your confession, I, as a called and ordained servant of the Word, announce the grace of God to all of you, and in the stead and by the command of my Lord Jesus Christ I forgive you all your sins in the name of the Father and of the Son and of the Holy Spirit.

Almighty God, our heavenly Father, has had mercy on us and has given his only Son to die for us and for his sake forgives us all our sins. To those who believe in his name he gives power to become the children of God and has promised them his Holy Spirit. He that believes and is baptized shall be saved. Grant this, Lord, to us all.

Lutheran Book of Worship

Almighty God, in his mercy, has given his Son to die for us and, for his sake, forgives us all our sins. As a called and ordained minister of the Church of Christ, and by his authority, I therefore declare to you the entire forgiveness of all your sins, in the name of the Father, and of the Son, and of the Holy Spirit.

In the mercy of almighty God, Jesus Christ was given to die for you, and for his sake God forgives you all your sins. To those who believe in Jesus Christ he gives the power to become the children of God and bestows on them the Holy Spirit.

5. *A congregational thanksgiving.* Quite often when a major congregational anniversary year is coming, the history of the congregation is researched and a story of its life is written. As part of the anniversary observance, a congregation might hold a service of thanksgiving that calls to mind important persons, groups, and events as manifestations of God's grace at work in that community of faith. Not only would this service build appreciation for how God has already been lovingly present in the congregation, it would strengthen confidence in God's abiding grace for facing the challenges of today.

6. *Questions for personal reflection and group discussion.* In case 1, Pastor Anderson seeks to bolster his sense of worth through work; in this way he relies upon himself rather than God. In what way do you resist God by trying to bolster your own sense of worth or security?

Like Sara in case 2, have you experienced a trial that tested your trust in God? How did you respond?

In reference to case 3, can you see ways in which your social or economic position in society influences your experience of God's grace?

In response to case 4, what is the most important meaning of God's grace for you?

4

RELIANCE ON
THE WORD OF GOD

I N THE LAST CHAPTER, we focused attention on trusting in God's grace, which is not just an idea but a living relationship. But where do we meet this gracious, loving God? Our pluralistic world is an open market where all sorts of individuals and groups are hawking their religious or spiritual wares. "Find God here." "Attain inner peace this way." "Discover your true self in this manner." In such a confusing situation, where do we meet God?

Some say that it doesn't matter that way we follow, for they all lead to God in any case. When one studies different religions and spiritualities in depth, however, one finds not only common ground here and there but also significant differences. For instance, ECKANKAR is an esoteric or New Age group that views God as the ultimate source of all things and the home that souls may finally reach with assistance from spiritual adepts such as the living ECK master. From this outlook, God is predominantly the distant goal that people should seek to find in a lofty nonmaterial realm. This is quite a different understanding of God than the biblical picture of God as the one who enters fully into this physical world to seek and to save the lost.

Others say that God is utter mystery, and each person or group just grasps a small portion of that mystery. This may seem very persuasive, for surely God is mysterious and beyond our comprehension. But if that is all we say, if God is utter mystery, how do we know that we can trust God? A mysterious reality is not necessarily kindly or even interested in us. Furthermore, in such a view, God is passive while humans try to figure out the divine puzzle. There is no revelation from God. God is distant and aloof.

The Lutheran tradition emphasizes the biblical understanding of God as the shepherd who seeks the lost sheep, the woman who searches for the lost coin. True, God is mystery, but the divine mystery is evident both in the strangeness of a love that sacrifices itself in Jesus and in the awesome power that creates this enormous universe. The God made known in the lengthy biblical story of Israel, Jesus, and the early church is not a passive, aloof God, but a God of love who initiates a relationship with people and seeks to draw them into an ever deeper bond. In this perspective, it is vital to consider the ways in which this God of grace comes to us. These are often called the *means of grace*.

God meets us in many ways—through significant individuals, our families, books, music, art, nature, social groups such as Christian congregations or Alcoholics Anonymous chapters. So in one sense there are a great many means of grace. But the Lutheran tradition has been especially concerned about where we may encounter the specific message of God's merciful grace—in other words, where we may be confident of coming across the gospel of Jesus Christ. In one of the Lutheran confessions, Martin Luther identifies these means of communicating the gospel: verbal proclamation, baptism, eucharist, absolution, and "mutual conversation and consolation of brethren."[1] These can be condensed into three means of grace: word, the sacraments of baptism and the Lord's supper, and confession/absolution. The word is the topic of this chapter; the sacraments of baptism and the Lord's supper and confession/absolution will be the topics of the next chapter.

Almost all Christian churches regard Word and Sacrament as the chief means of grace. However, they have differed on whether word or sacrament is more prominent. Lutheranism is one of those traditions that has viewed word as the primary means of grace. We get an initial sense of what this involves by simply comparing common practices in a typical Roman Catholic church with those in a typical Lutheran church. At a Roman Catholic church, every worship service includes eucharist and has a sermon or homily that probably lasts seven to ten minutes. At a typical Lutheran church, the Sunday morning worship service has a sermon that lasts fifteen to twenty minutes and eucharist may or may not be celebrated. While Roman Catholic practice indicates that the eucharist is more important than the sermon, Lutheran practice suggests that the sermon is more important.

This Lutheran accent on the sermon is part of a broader emphasis on words as the primary means by which God communicates with human beings and builds up the relationship of trust in God. Along with words in preaching and other forms of oral testimony, Lutherans have stressed words in the Bible and singing. Thus we may state the third characteristic of Lutheran spirituality as reliance on the word of God in Scripture, proclamation, and singing as the primary source of spiritual nurture and guidance.

It's important to understand that *word of God* is a metaphor for communication or revelation from God. We use *word* in a similar sense when we ask someone, "What's the word?" Here *word* means message or communication. Thus in a general sense, word of God is a message or revelation from God. Christians have commonly distinguished three forms of the *word of God:* Jesus Christ himself (Word of God), the Bible, and oral proclamation of the biblical message. In turn we will consider these forms and also include the word in song.

JESUS CHRIST AS WORD OF GOD

In a preeminent way, Jesus Christ is the Word of God. This is affirmed at the beginning of the Gospel of John. "In the beginning was the Word, and the Word was with God, and the Word was God. He was in the beginning with God. All things came into being through him. . . . And the Word became flesh and lived among us" (John 1:1-3, 14). Think what this implies. First, it claims that the one who "became flesh and lived among us" as Jesus is God and the one who has created all things. We could spend a lifetime and never exhaust the meaning of this. Second and more to our present purpose, to rely on the word of God is to rely on the person of Jesus Christ. So fundamentally, reliance on the word of God is not about accepting a certain idea, or theory, but about a personal relationship with Christ. In the preceding chapter, we said that trust in the merciful grace of God is basically a relationship of confidence in God. Now we are simply looking at another side of this same relationship. For Christians, trusting in the merciful grace of God and relying on Jesus Christ are simply different ways of talking about the same personal relationship. Part of what is added by saying Jesus is the Word of God is that his life, teachings, suffering, death, and resurrection become the central message that God wants to communicate to humans.

Now we must consider two qualities of the word of God that are emphasized in the Lutheran tradition. One quality is that the word of God comes in two forms—*law and gospel.* This holds whether the word of God is Jesus Christ, Scripture, or oral proclamation. One way God communicates is to issue commandments and moral teachings that convey what human beings ought to be and do. Clear examples come from the Ten Commandments, "You shall not murder. You shall not commit adultery. You shall not steal" (Exodus 20:13-15). And from the teachings of Jesus, "You shall love the Lord your God with all your heart, and with all your soul, and with all your mind" (Matthew 22:37). While law is useful for maintaining some degree of order in society, the main spiritual function of divine commands is to make us aware of our sin. We may not have violated "You shall not murder," but we all fall short of loving God with all our heart, soul, and mind. The law tends to undermine confidence in our own resources. When we take the law to heart, we have less trust in our own strength and virtue.

The other way God communicates is through the gospel. The gospel expresses what God does for the world, what God gives to people, above all, in Jesus Christ. A well-known statement of gospel is John 3:16, "For God so loved the world that he gave his only Son, so that everyone who believes in him may not perish but may have eternal life." But there is also gospel in the Old Testament such as the prophet's message to the Israelites suffering exile in Babylon, "Comfort, O comfort my people, says your God" (Isaiah 40:1). In short, gospel declares the grace or gifts of God.

It is important to see that God speaks in both ways—in law and gospel. Through law God's highest purpose is to awaken us more fully to our need for God. This does not happen in a moment, for we are persistent in our tendency to rely upon our own resources. Through the gospel God seeks to arouse and strengthen our trust in the divine goodness and mercy. Thus both law and gospel are part of the word of God.

A second quality of a Lutheran understanding of the word of God is what Luther calls "the theology of the cross"; it is closely linked with the distinction between law and gospel. Luther recognized that there is a measure of divine revelation in nature and human morality, for there we can see aspects of God's law. However, since sinful human beings are alienated from God, they misinterpret such revelation. Hence, if people form their conception of God chiefly from observations about nature and morality, they will have a distorted view of God as one who is chiefly lawgiver. Luther says that we can only come to know God truly through the gospel and especially the revelation given in the cross of Jesus. This runs contrary to our usual thinking, for we expect the almighty God to be manifest in deeds of power in history and in our own lives. But Luther says that we come to know God most truly in suffering, both in the life of Jesus and in our own lives.

We can restate Luther's theology of the cross this way. Sure, we may have insights into God that are linked with moments of beauty in nature, moral teachings, and thoughts from various religious and philosophical thinkers. Such perceptions have their own limited value, but the problem is that we tend to trust overly much in them. Frequently we learn the inadequacy of such views of God when suffering strikes in our lives. Then we may get angry with God, even lose our faith, for God has not done what we thought God ought to do. Luther says that if we look carefully at the cross of Jesus, then we discover a different God, one who is most deeply revealed in weakness, suffering, and death. The events of Jesus' life show that he was not protected from opposition, rejection, tribulation, and death. In the end, to be sure, God does overcome evil in the resurrection of Jesus. But the path to the glory of resurrection is through suffering. Since God dealt that way with Jesus, we should not expect anything different. God will not shield us from all sorrow and pain; at some points in our lives, we will have to endure them. This might lead us to think God is uncaring or mean, a distant sovereign who merely watches people suffer. But Luther and the heart of the Christian tradition say that rather than being a cold, aloof ruler, Jesus shows us that God shares in our suffering. The crucial point is that the suffering, death, and resurrection of

Jesus not only tell us something about this particular good man, they tell us something profound and mysterious *about God and God's ways with us.* God may not bring us deliverance from trouble, but will share the trouble with us. This contradicts our usual way of thinking in which we expect God to ward off everything bad. It is a wrenching experience to have our understanding of God (and of ourselves) so drastically challenged. Yet what may emerge from such a painful time is a more refined, deepened trust in God. There is less confidence in our own strength, virtue, and understanding. As we are made more humble, we also become more willing to rely upon God.

In summary, we can say that the central reality of relying upon the word of God is the personal relationship of trusting in Jesus Christ. Both law and gospel point to this center and especially to the cross of Jesus that helps us trust in God even in the midst of suffering.

THE WORD OF GOD
IN SCRIPTURE AND PROCLAMATION

In practice, Lutheranism has held that the primary way of relating to Jesus Christ is through human words that testify to Jesus. Such human words are found especially in the written words of the Bible and in the spoken words of biblically based witness. We will look at both of these.

While Jesus Christ is the Word of God or divine communication in the fullest sense, we cannot book a flight to Palestine for face-to-face meeting with Jesus. We who live after the earthly lifetime of Jesus have access to him through the testimony of those who believed in him. At first this testimony was given in oral form by such people as Mary Magdalene, Peter, and Paul, but within a few decades written testimonies circulated in the churches. Not until the last half of the fourth century was nearly universal agreement reached about which writings should form the New Testament. The New Testament and the Old Testament make up Scripture, the holy writings that are the canon, or standard texts, for Christian teaching.[2]

One of the watchwords of Lutheranism has been *sola Scriptura,* that is, Scripture alone is recognized as the authoritative source and norm of preaching, teaching, and practice. Here there is a significant, although sometimes overdrawn, contrast with the Scripture and tradition stance taken by the Roman Catholic Church at the Council of Trent, which accepts church tradition as a source of authoritative teaching that may go beyond what is in Scripture, but may not contradict Scripture. It is possible to exaggerate the difference between these two outlooks, for surely Lutherans use church tradition in their interpretation of the Bible. The Augsburg Confession recognizes three ancient creeds, especially the Apostles' and Nicene, as authentic interpretations of biblical faith. And because Lutheran churches regard the Lutheran confessions as faithful interpretations of scripture, those churches also use the confessions as guides in the understanding of Scripture. Nonetheless, in principle, for Lutherans Scripture always stands above anything else in church tradition. And Lutherans refuse to endorse teachings that they believe have no substantial support in Scripture, such as two Roman Catholic doctrines about Mary: the Immaculate Conception and Bodily Assumption.

The nature of Scriptural authority has been debated among Lutherans. One very influential view has been that since "all scripture is inspired by God" (2 Timothy 3:16; cf 2 Peter 1:21; 1 Corinthians 2:13), the Bible is inerrant. To say that Scripture is inspired by God is understood to mean the Holy Spirit taught the very words used by the biblical writers. In a strict sense, then, the words of the Bible *are* the word of God. This gives the Bible a certain authority. Because God inspired these authors in this way long ago, we *ought* to believe the Scriptures. Yet this view also says that what gives the Bible actual authority for a person today is when the Holy Spirit works effectively through Scripture to create and nurture faith in Christ.[3] The clearest articulation of this position in the older Lutheran tradition was by seventeenth-century Lutheran orthodox theologians.

Another view affirms that God inspired the biblical authors to witness faithfully to divine revelation, but says this does not necessarily mean the Bible is inerrant. This perspective puts the heaviest accent on what the Holy Spirit accomplishes through the biblical words in the present. Thus it stresses that the Bible becomes authoritative for persons or groups when God conveys a message through its words today. This outlook may admit that there are some discrepancies in the Bible, but the Holy Spirit makes use of occasionally fallible human words to communicate God's truth. The point emphasized is that the words of the Bible *become* the word of God.

Proponents of this perspective point to Martin Luther for support. In a brief preface to his translation of the New Testament Epistle of James, Luther says he thinks the book is not written by an apostle, because it ascribes justification to works and does not preach Christ: "What does not teach Christ is not apostolic, not even if taught by Peter or Paul. . . . I therefore refuse him a place among the writers of the true canon of my Bible."[4] Here Luther shows that for him the gospel of Jesus Christ and justification by faith are the keys to interpreting the Bible, and by that standard James is deficient. In fact, in Bibles that used Luther's translation and editing, until around 1600, the Epistle of James was published as an unnumbered appendix.

Although there are differences between these two views about the nature of divine inspiration of the biblical authors, both agree that what gives Scripture authority in the lives of people is that God speaks to them through the Scriptural words today. It matters little what people's *theory* of biblical inspiration is, if they never read or reflect on the Bible's words. What counts is that they listen for God's message in and through Scripture. For instance, when a tragic death occurs in a family, if family members read or recall some words of Scripture to help pour out their grief and seek God's comfort, then the Bible truly has genuine influence in their lives.

Just as trust in any relationship is built up over time, so trust in Scripture grows with experience. As we go through life, if we find the words of Scripture illuminating our path, giving voice to our joy, expressing our anger, and consoling us in sorrow, then step by step our confidence in the written word of God increases. Slowly we learn that the Bible is an inexhaustible source of spiritual nourishment.

While the written word of the Bible is precious, Luther regarded oral proclamation of the word as the primary means for communicating the gospel. He said, "The Church is not a pen house, but a mouth house. . . . Christ Himself has not written anything, nor has He ordered anything to be written, but rather to be preached by word of mouth."[5] Luther called preaching, "the best and most necessary part of the mass."[6] Sermons are so central for Christian worship that Luther says Christians should never gather for worship without preaching. "Therefore, when God's word is not preached, one had better neither sing nor read, or even come together. "[7] So ever since the beginning, most Lutherans have regarded the sermon as the high point of the worship service.

But not just any preaching will do. Preaching must be based on the Bible. To encourage preaching on the breadth of Scripture, Lutheran preachers normally draw their sermons from a series of biblical texts for the church year called a lectionary. Furthermore, there has been an effort over the years to hire educated pastors whose preparation includes thorough study of the Bible using the original New Testament language of Greek, and often Hebrew for the Old Testament as well.

Formal preaching is not the only, or even the most important, way in which the word of God is orally declared. Less public but probably more weighty testimony takes place when parents share their faith and pray with their children. Proclamation also happens in classes and other conversations where the Christian message is spoken, as well as when people sing hymns or spiritual songs.

Attentiveness to the Word

While Bible and oral proclamation are fundamental as presentations of the word that are objective, or outside of us, various forms of response to the word complete the other, more subjective, side of the picture. The appropriate response is faithful attentiveness to the word of God. Luther speaks of this attentiveness in a sermon when he says observing a holy day such as Sunday, is to "concern yourself with the Word of God, devote yourself to it at home and especially in church." So he says, "Take heed that you do not despise the preaching and neglect the Word of God! Secondly, see to it that you speak of it seriously, hear it, sing it, read it, use it, and learn it!"[8] In short, Luther calls for faithful attentiveness to the word of God, whether that word be in a sermon, a scripture reading at church or home, a liturgical response, a hymn, or words recalled at any time.

Luther's primary stress is on the objective power of the word itself. "When we seriously ponder the word, hear it, and put it to use, such is its power that it never departs without fruit. It always awakens new understanding, new pleasure, and a new spirit of devotion, and it constantly cleanses the heart and its meditations. For these words are not idle or dead, but effective and living."[9] What makes these words "effective and living" is when Christ speaks in and through them to a person or community. Or to say the same thing in another way, human words become the word of God when the Holy Spirit uses them to communicate with someone. Thus it is God who continually initiates communication with us.

Secondarily, though, attentiveness to the word of God on our part is important. Luther points to this above, saying, "When we seriously ponder the Word, hear it, and put it to use . . .". There are many ways of being attentive to the word. Lutherans have traditionally focused upon attendance at worship and some forms of pondering Scripture, but in recent years many have also employed approaches cultivated in other Christian traditions. We shall look at these ways in turn.

First, part of being attentive to the word is to participate in corporate worship services and to be alert to the word in the sermon and other parts of the service such as the liturgy, Scripture readings, and hymns. Whereas watching television conditions us to be passive and expect something outside us to excite our interest, being awake to the word in worship is an active stance. Mere bodily presence at worship is not sufficient; listening for the word within the words is important. Thus the attitude with which we approach worship has a significant effect upon what happens there for us.

Second, certain methods of pondering Scripture have been staples among Lutherans. Chief among these has been *meditation on the Bible*. To meditate on a portion of the Bible is to listen for what God has to say to us in our current situation through these particular words. According to Martin Luther, meditation on the words of Scripture is the key to prayer. This comes out clearly in the reformer's advice to his barber about prayer in which Luther says to begin prayer by reciting or reading some portion of Scripture or the Apostles' Creed that summarizes Scripture. His point is that the word of God warms the heart to prayer.[10] In other words, prayer is not just our speaking to God, but is also listening to God. Prayer is communication that moves in two directions—from God to us and from us to God. Listening for the word of God within the words of the Bible is essentially what Christian meditation on Scripture is all about. Various patterns for this have been followed. Luther often began with a part of the catechism such as the Lord's Prayer, Ten Commandments, or Apostles' Creed. Others have centered meditation on one or more of the biblical texts appointed for each day in a lectionary. Some have used devotional works in which a major component has been a portion of Scripture and some reflections on it such as John Arndt's devotional classic *True Christianity*, the still popular Moravian *Daily Texts*, and contemporary booklets such as *Christ in Our Home*. A 1994 four-volume book that brings together several sources for devotions over a two-year period is *For All the Saints*, which provides for each day an opening prayer, three Scripture readings, a reading from a saint like C. S. Lewis, and a closing prayer.[11]

Another way Lutherans have pondered Scripture is *Bible study*. To study the Bible is a different stance than to meditate on it. When we study, our mind is probing, asking questions. We are active, largely in control. When we meditate on Scripture, we are more receptive, less in control, more open to whatever may come. Study is rather like carrying on an interrogation, while meditation is essentially listening to whatever is said. Nevertheless, the border between study and meditation on the Bible is often crossed. Many times an insight gained from study of Scripture leads into thoughtful reflection on its implications for one's life—in short, to meditation. In the last several decades in the United States, many Lutheran congregations have benefited from well-organized Bible study programs with printed guides. Historically Luther's Small Catechism has been used for both study and meditation, although that practice has declined considerably in recent years.

Third, especially since the 1970s, some Lutherans have appropriated ways of being attentive to the word of God that have been more widely practiced in other Christian traditions, including the Eastern Orthodox, Anglican, and Roman Catholic traditions. One such practice is the *spiritual retreat*. Frequently what Lutherans label a retreat is really a workshop conducted at a different location. Whereas a workshop has a schedule that is just as busy or even busier than one's daily life, a true spiritual retreat has a relaxed pace that is conducive to rest, worship, meditation, and just being in God's presence. The spiritual retreat is a time for disengagement from one's usual schedule in order to concentrate attention on one's relationship with God and its meaning for daily life.

Another experience that some Lutherans are entering into is one-to-one *spiritual direction*. This is usually a relationship with a trusted person with whom one can reflect on one's relationship with God. Spiritual direction is not the same as counseling, for the focus in spiritual direction is on prayer and overall association with God. Thus the heart of spiritual direction for the Christian is to attend to the word of God as it impinges on one's life. Spiritual direction most often occurs in a periodic, perhaps monthly, meeting, but it can also take place in daily sessions during a spiritual retreat. Sometimes the spiritual director will suggest some passages of Scripture for meditation between conferences.[12]

Contemplative prayer is also a way of being attentive to the word, although in a different manner than in conversational prayer. We can distinguish three dimensions of prayer: listening to God (meditation), speaking to God, and attending to God's presence. Contemplative prayer is attention to the presence of God. The divine presence is usually mediated by words or images; so when we listen and speak to God, often we also are aware of God's presence. In fact, the divine presence can be so strong that a person may feel very close to God. Martin Luther speaks in this way of the believer being united by faith with Christ. Thus there is a contemplative dimension present within a great deal of prayer. Yet the contemplative dimension of prayer is most evident on those occasions when Christ's presence is sensed even though words and images recede or even disappear. For the Christian, contemplative prayer is an intimate form of communion with Christ the Word of God.[13]

THE WORD OF GOD IN MUSIC

Since music has been an especially prominent way of being attentive to the word of God in the Lutheran tradition, it deserves separate discussion. Music serves both to express people's faith and to form their faith. Our focus will be on the formative side of music, that is, how God's grace works in and through music to establish and shape

Christian faith. No one fully understands why music has such a powerful effect on human beings, but we can distinguish three significant elements in music's influence on us. First, music often awakens our feelings. Of course, words may also touch us deeply, so a particular combination of words and music may be especially moving. Second, music is symbolic; that is, it may point to a meaning that eludes straightforward description. Since words too may be symbolic, a happy blend of words and music may very effectively express profound meaning. Third, music may have a rhythm that invites a physical response such as swaying, tapping a foot, or dancing. Here, too, words and music may reinforce one another. All together, then, the word of God may have a very effective impact on people through music, for music can convey the rich meanings of the Christian message in such a way that it touches people's hearts and even involves their whole bodies.

Music was prominent in the worship and devotional life of the Israelites and early Christians. We do not know the tunes used in ancient times, because a system for writing down music was not invented until the eleventh century C.E. Yet there are ample references to the use of musical instruments and songs in the Old Testament and New Testament. Early in Israel's history, dance was an accepted part of worship. King David was even criticized by his wife Michal for his enthusiastic dancing while taking the ark of the covenant to Jerusalem (2 Samuel 6:15-23). The psalms were sung in both the temple and the synagogues. The early Christians took over the synagogue practice of singing psalms and added other hymns of praise to God. By the fourth century, though, Christians had come to generally avoid dancing and instrumental music in worship, because dance and music were linked with immoral practices in the culture of that time. During the Middle Ages, the chief form of music used in worship was the Gregorian chant that had a single line of melody without any accompaniment. Participation was limited by the fact that the mass was in Latin, which only the learned understood. In addition, gradually more laypeople were further left out of singing by complexities introduced into the music. Here we see a tension between the desires of the trained musician and the musically untrained congregation. The total result was that prior to the Reformation, singing in church was performed mostly by the priest, choir, and monastic communities; the laity listened.[14]

An important part of Martin Luther's movement to reform the church involved music. One aspect of his reform was to involve the congregation more fully in the worship service through singing the liturgy either in Latin, for churches with many who understood the language, or in the everyday language. Luther enlisted the aid of skilled musicians to help him compose music for the liturgy that would fit with the German language. In addition, Luther revived the ancient practice of congregational hymn singing.[15] Luther himself wrote a number of hymns and encouraged others to do so. These reforms arose in part from Luther's recognition of the power of music to touch human emotions. He said, "Next to the Word of God, music deserves the highest praise. She is a mistress and governess of those human emotions . . . which as masters govern men or more often overwhelm them. . . . For whether you wish to comfort the sad, to terrify the happy, to encourage the despairing . . . what more effective means than music could you find?"[16]

Luther's positive view of music contrasts with the attitude of some other reformers who were wary of the power of music and the arts to sway people. For many years the Reformed tradition followed John Calvin's opinion that only psalm singing should be permitted in Christian worship. Luther expressed a more positive outlook, "Nor am I of the opinion that the gospel should destroy and blight all the arts, as some of the pseudo-religious claim. . . . But I would like to see all the arts, especially music, used in the service of Him who gave and made them."[17] While music had a prominent place in Lutheran worship, for about a century congregations sang in unison and without accompaniment. The choir might have sung in parts, and the organ or other instruments might have accompanied the choir or played between stanzas sung by congregation and choir. Gradually the organ came to play along with congregational singing.

For several centuries, music flourished in the Lutheran churches of Germany. The number of fine hymns greatly increased, and much outstanding music was composed for choir, organ, and other instruments. For special occasions, there were lengthy musical treatments of biblical stories called oratorios; Handel's *Messiah* is the best known oratorio. The great seventeenth-century German composer Heinrich Schutz wrote numerous musical renditions of biblical texts for small choirs and even large-scale productions for multiple choirs. Johann Sebastian Bach followed with many compositions for organ, more than 300 cantatas (shorter than oratorios) that gave musical interpretation of poems based on biblical texts, and other creations based on biblical events and the liturgy of the mass. In short, the Lutheran tradition was strong both in congregational singing of liturgy and hymns and in listening to special music for choir, organ, and other instruments. This emphasis on both singing and listening is still evident in many larger Lutheran churches in Germany today where a full-time cantor is responsible not only for leading congregational singing with the organ but also for directing choirs and composing music for original local presentations on biblical themes. It is also by no means accidental that many Lutheran colleges in the United States today have large, high-quality music departments and outstanding choirs.

One of the perennial tensions in church music generally, as well as among Lutherans, is between art music and congregational music, that is, between music that satisfies the trained artist and music that involves the ordinary congregation that has few skills. There is certainly a place for the occasional grand musical production such as Handel's *Messiah* that calls for orchestra, fine soloists, and well-rehearsed chorus. While this work is far beyond the resources of a typical congregation to produce, ordinary people generally find it a moving experience in listening. On the other hand, a steady diet of music that met such high standards would leave all but a few churchgoers as listeners only. The tension between art music and congregational music is also evident in hymns. The text of a hymn cannot be difficult to grasp and its music cannot be very demanding, or else the common Christian will be left out. Some hymns meet the needs of everyone. But frequently there has been a division between the hymns that musicians think appropriate for Sunday worship and the songs that many Lutherans love to sing in Sunday school or at camp. While these beloved songs have been passed on in special songbooks, they have mostly been excluded from Lutheran hymnals.[18]

Closely related to the tension between art music and congregational music is the tension between what is considered Lutheran and the music of a people's own culture. That is, sometimes what has been considered truly Lutheran music are classic German chorales and especially Luther's hymns sung in the rhythmic way he wrote them. For North American Lutherans of European origin, this has often meant that songs from their pietist roots in Europe, gospel songs from revivalistic movements, and new songs from the charismatic movement are frowned upon. Objections are sometimes rightly raised to the words of a song as lacking Christian substance, but frequently the music itself is criticized as unsuitable for Lutheran worship. At the same time, Lutherans have bemoaned the loss of members to churches that have embraced the music of the culture.[19] The same question arises in relation to the musical forms of jazz, folk, pop, rock, and country western. Are these suitable music styles for Lutheran worship? Although many songs in these styles lack the rich symbolic depth of great music and verse, they often connect with people's feelings and have a beat that invites them to move their bodies.

Lutherans of other ethnic groups deal with the same tension between what is considered Lutheran and the music of their culture. For instance, the centrality of music in the traditional African cultures in northern Tanzania fits well with Lutheranism's emphasis on music, yet if Tanzanian Lutherans in Arusha were limited to the chorales brought by German missionaries, Christianity would not sink deeply into their lives. As it is, these Africans both sing European hymns and move their feet while singing African tunes, sometimes accompanied by drums or keyboard. African American Lutherans likewise deal with a dual heritage of European Lutheranism and elements in their own culture such as call and response, the holler, the shout, and black gospel music.[20] Latino Lutherans face a comparable situation. While the members of Iglesia Todos los Santos in Minneapolis do the traditional Lutheran liturgy, they sing it with Latin music accompanied by a small band strong on percussion. The songs are also Latin in style, with a heavy beat that inspires toe tapping and periodic clapping. As their pastor, J. Antonio Machado, says, "Latino people live more in their bodies than do Northern Europeans." This is evident in the ease with which old and young alike move their bodies with the music.

The fundamental point in all of this is that music in the church is meant to serve the word of God. Music has the power to enhance attentiveness to the word, so that faith may be fed. Given the tremendous diversity of people, there should be diversity of music in the church. There is a place for various forms of art music in the Lutheran Church. The richness of the word deserves our most profound musical expression. There is also a store of fine hymns that continue to nurture faith. On the other hand, presenting the word in a musical form that connects with people is what counts most of all. Not everyone resonates with Bach or even the English hymns of Charles Wesley, but some may feel a tie with a jazz or country western version of a song or hymn. As Gracia Grindal says, "We have to make connection with the old songs, without becoming museum curators, and also greeters of the new songs that have suddenly become our old favorites. We can work to make all of our churches places where people of all stripes do, on occasion, hear their song."[21] Living with such diversity of music requires that we love one another. What counts above all else is that music helps us rely on the word of God in life and in death.

To summarize, in this chapter we began with the question, Where is the merciful grace of God made known to us? While God is surely present at all times and places, Christians believe God's loving goodness is revealed most fully in Jesus Christ. Martin Luther identified basically three means by which God's grace in Christ is communicated: word, sacrament, and confession/absolution. As the eternal Word of God, Jesus Christ speaks to people today through human words—in Scripture and diverse forms of oral testimony. The Lutheran tradition relies on the word of God as the primary means of spiritual nurture. There is no one universal way among Lutherans for achieving attentiveness to the word of God, but cultivation of some such practices is essential for nourishing faith.

For Reflection and Practice

1. *Active listening to the worship service.* Listening is not quite the same thing as hearing. Sometimes we hear things that we do not want to hear, such as a sudden loud noise. Other times we listen for something but never hear it. Listening is the attempt to hear. Whereas hearing can be quite passive, listening is an active stance. The same difference is found between seeing and looking. Whether we use the aural or visual metaphor, listening and looking both involve attentiveness. To be attentive to the word of God in worship means to be an active listener.

a. Reflect on your last experience at a worship service. What was your frame of mind when the service began? Were you harried and preoccupied or were you calm and focused on what would come? What was going on in your life at the time? Did anything in the service speak to you? Why? In your opinion, to what extent does meaningful worship depend on factors outside you? Inside you? If you are part of a group, share your thoughts with one another. If you are in a large group, share first in subgroups of three to four persons.

b. Group exercise. Agree to meet with others after weekly worship for perhaps four to six weeks, in order to discuss the sermon for that day. Focus your discussion on what the sermon said to you. Do this first in small groups of three or four. Stay close to your actual experience with the sermon. Try to avoid theorizing and saying what you think ought to have happened. Report what did in fact happen for you. Recall what was happening in your life at the time. When you come together as a total group, briefly describe the responses in each subgroup. Now reflect together, What accounts for the diverse responses to the very same sermon? As the group proceeds through the weeks, ask what we as listeners can do to help make the sermon a time when the word of God touches us. Do people become more connected with one another as they realize that a sermon that does not speak to them may speak to others?

2. *Meditation on Scripture:* lectio divina. Luther's personal form of meditation on the Lord's Prayer, Ten Commandments, and Apostles' Creed resembles a yet older form called *lectio divina,* which literally

means "divine reading." In this approach, one first reads a portion of Scripture once and then rereads it slowly, and when a word or phrase stands out, one dwells on it, turning it over in one's mind. The word or phrase makes associations with one's life, and often in response one speaks to God. In practice, reading the Bible in this way involves a person in these dimensions of prayer: meditation, or listening to what God says through the biblical passage; speaking to God in response; and sometimes contemplation in which one simply rests in the presence of God with few or no words.

Meditate on Psalm 130 using the approach of *lectio divina*. This psalm is a poignant hymn of attentiveness to God expressed in waiting and hoping in God. Allow ten to fifteen minutes. Sit comfortably upright with both feet on the floor. Remember to read through the whole psalm once, and then reread it slowly; stop to ponder a word or phrase that speaks to you. If you become aware of wandering off in your thoughts, return to the psalm and read again until a word or phrase strikes you. If you are in a group, have someone charged in advance to end the time of prayer with an Amen or a soft bell. In gatherings of three to four persons, share what happened during your meditation. Be honest. Finally come together as a total assembly to deal with any questions or thoughts that people wish to discuss.

3. *The Jesus prayer.* A form of prayer that is conducive to contemplative prayer is the ancient Jesus prayer that has been especially nurtured in the Eastern Orthodox tradition. The prayer consists of these words, "Lord Jesus Christ, have mercy on me." One slowly repeats the words silently or out loud. You may find it helpful to correlate the prayer with your breathing, thinking "Lord Jesus Christ" as you inhale and "have mercy on me" as you exhale. Besides the symbolism of this action, it may assist you to relax. Set aside ten minutes for the prayer. Sit comfortably upright with both feet on the floor, and begin to repeat the words of the prayer. Your thoughts may stray off to "business" matters or trivial things. When you become aware of that, just gently return to the Jesus prayer. You will likely find that at first your mind is busy with lots of other thoughts, but if you keep coming back to the Jesus prayer, you will probably settle down after several minutes into a quiet, restful state. You may discover that the prayer will shorten, so

that you are only thinking "Lord Jesus Christ" or just "Jesus." It may also be that your thoughts never settle down, and you find the prayer unsatisfying. That is OK. This type of prayer suits some people but not others. If a number of you are doing this, share your experience with the prayer in groups of three to four persons. Don't be afraid to report what actually happened, for it may be helpful to someone else. Then allow some time for the entire group to talk about the prayer.

4. *Meditation on a hymn or song.* Hymns and spiritual songs are fertile ground for meditation. Choose one of your favorite hymns or spiritual songs from a book. Read its stanzas and dwell on those words or lines that speak to you most powerfully. Do you find that sometimes the tune of a hymn or spiritual song repeats itself in your mind? This is a type of spontaneous prayer. If you do this with others, after a time of meditation, come together in clusters of three to four to share from your reflections. Some time together as a whole group is also advisable.

5. *Meditation with recorded music.* Various forms of music help us disengage from worries and focus on God. Music stores and religious bookshops have CD and tape recordings of great religious art music, hymns, high-quality meditative music from the Taize ecumenical community in France, as well as pop-style praise music from charismatic and Evangelical groups. For personal meditation or for a period of quiet with a group, play the music. For an individual or group, this can serve as a way to begin a session that employs other forms of meditation also.

6. *Reflection and discussion on music in your congregation.* If you are part of a large group, divide first into subgroups of three to four people to foster wider participation. Discuss the following questions: (a) What music in recent worship services spoke to you or enhanced worship? (Remember that this includes liturgy, hymns or songs, choir anthems, and pieces by organ or other instruments.) Why was that music meaningful to you? (b) Are there ways music might better serve the word of God in your worship services? (c) Is there sufficient diversity of music in your congregation's worship services? Are there people who feel left out?

5

MEETING GOD IN PHYSICAL SYMBOLS

WHERE DO WE MEET THE MERCIFUL GRACE OF GOD? This is the very practical and urgent issue that we began to address in the previous chapter. The first answer to this question given by the Lutheran tradition is that the God of mercy meets us in words—and centrally in words that speak of ancient Israel and Jesus, the word or message of God. Now we must look at the second part of the answer, namely, that this word/message of God also meets us in material things and bodily gestures that speak symbolically of divine grace.

We are very familiar with physical objects and bodily gestures having symbolic meaning. In many cultures, wedding couples exchange rings as a symbol of marital union. On other special occasions, people often present a gift as a token of esteem and affection. When we meet one another, we not only speak, but also make gestures of greeting common in our culture: perhaps a certain hand movement, bow, or smile. When we express love for another person, in addition to words, we hug or kiss. As physical beings, we use physical means to communicate with one another. Even our communication with words has physical components of sound or visual marks. But these sounds and visual markings of language are different, for they can be linked together in a wide variety of ways. Nonlinguistic physical symbols and bodily gestures operate on a different level of significance than words and have their own power.

Potentially God may encounter us through any material thing in the world. For example, the age and sturdiness of a large oak tree may remind us of God's eternal being. Or some soil might make us think of our Creator's provision for life on earth. However, the tree and soil do not tell us about the merciful grace of God that shares our suffering, forgives our shortcomings, and grounds our hope for life beyond death. The fullest and surest source of that message, say Christians, is the life, death, and resurrection of Jesus. Christians believe that God has communicated with humans most fully in and through the bodily life of this human being. So Jesus is the fundamental physical symbol of God.[1] Furthermore, physical symbols that are closely linked to Jesus may speak to us about God's grace in him. It's clear that Jesus himself communicated through material objects and bodily gestures. For instance, he used mud and water in giving sight to a blind man (John 9:6-7) and employed laying on of hands as well as words to heal a crippled woman (Luke 13:10-13).

In the New Testament, we are told that Jesus especially endorsed two actions involving physical symbols—baptism and the Lord's supper. Jesus commands his followers to baptize and celebrate the Lord's supper, and he promises certain blessings in connection with these two actions involving physical objects. Thus while a number of material things may be symbols of God's merciful grace, the fact that Jesus especially approved baptism and the Lord's supper gives assurance that God meets us there.

The term most Christians use for these rites with a physical symbol is sacrament, although Eastern Orthodox Christians call them a mystery. The New Testament does not specify the number of sacraments or mysteries; in fact, the word *sacrament* does not even occur there. So Christians have differed on how many sacraments they recognize. Augustine thought there is an indefinite number of sacraments. While he regarded baptism and the Lord's supper as foremost, in his view making the sign of the cross or giving salt to a person in baptism are also sacraments. This fluid thinking about the number of sacraments began to change in the twelfth century when the influential theologian Peter Lombard said there are seven sacraments: baptism, the Lord's supper, penance, confirmation, anointing for healing, ordination, and marriage. Over the next several centuries, this became official Roman Catholic doctrine.

The Lutheran confessions give somewhat mixed testimony about the number of things to be called sacraments, because Luther and

Melanchthon define the term differently. On the one hand, Martin Luther challenged the official teaching of seven sacraments and said there are only two—baptism and the Lord's supper. Luther defined a sacrament as a physical sign accompanied by Jesus' explicit promise and command. For a time, Luther was unsure about confession and absolution (penance), but he finally ruled it out as a sacrament because it lacked a physical sign to go along with its clear biblical words of promise. Nonetheless, since the announcement of God's mercy in Christ to the repentant sinner is so central to the gospel, Luther said that "confession and absolution should by no means be allowed to fall into disuse in the church."[2]

On the other hand, Melanchthon defined a sacrament as "rites which have the command of God and to which the promise of grace has been added." According to this definition, a sacrament need not have a physical symbol. Hence Melanchthon proceeds to identify as sacraments not only baptism, the Lord's supper, and absolution, but also prayer, alms, and afflictions.[3] The difference in terminology is not so crucial, for the Lutheran confessions fully agree that confession and absolution is a means of grace endorsed by Jesus. Even though it is usually not called a sacrament, its importance and regular use are repeatedly underscored in the confessions.[4]

Nearly all Protestant groups followed Luther in recognizing only two sacraments, although the Salvation Army and most Quakers have no sacraments. Today churches continue to differ on the number of sacraments. The Eastern Orthodox and Roman Catholic Churches recognize seven; most Protestant churches two. Nevertheless, all these agree that baptism and the Lord's supper are the chief sacraments, and the other five that Roman Catholic and Eastern Orthodox churches call sacraments are observed as sacred rites in the Lutheran church. For Lutheran spirituality, baptism, the Lord's supper, and confession/absolution have profound and potentially far-reaching significance. We shall consider each ritual in turn.

BAPTISM

Baptism is an action that douses a person with water in connection with the name of Jesus or the triune God of Father, Son, and Holy

Spirit. In his Small Catechism, Luther emphasizes, "Baptism is not merely water, but it is water used according to God's command and connected with God's Word."[5] The word of God so connected is first of all Jesus' command in Matthew 28:19, "Go therefore, and make disciples of all nations, baptizing them in the name of the Father and of the Son and of the Holy Spirit." In addition to these words, though, the Word of God is also Jesus Christ himself. There is a strong sense that God is present in and through the water and words of baptism. While this is a presence that commands baptism, it is primarily a presence that promises blessings. In the simple words and actions of baptism, God promises blessings to the one baptized.

Using water in this manner is symbolic of the promised blessings. Luther and Lutherans stress two blessings that are promised and symbolized in baptism. One is cleansing. Since human beings all over the world use water to wash themselves, washing in God's name is a natural symbol for cleansing from sin. Reference is made to this in Acts 22:16, "And now why do you delay? Get up, be baptized, and have your sins washed away, calling on his name." So baptism is symbolic of God's promise to forgive sins.

A second, less obvious symbolic promise of baptism is underscored in the letters of Paul: dying and rising with Christ. In the early church, those baptized were generally dunked under water and then brought up again. The action of dunking represents drowning, and Paul connects this with Christ's death. The person baptized dies symbolically or metaphorically with Christ. Paul says the one baptized has died to sin. Being brought up out of the water signifies Christ's resurrection and the Christian's entrance into a new life of faithfulness to God (see Romans 6).[6]

These two meanings of baptism correspond to the two aspects of justification in Lutheran theology. That is, the first and fundamental aspect of justification is full forgiveness; we can also speak of this as God's complete acceptance of a person. The other aspect of justification is God's work of transforming persons so that they turn away from relying upon their own resources and seeking their own advantage and begin to trust in God and seek the welfare of others. This second dimension is also called sanctification. We recall that God's grace works simultaneously in both ways—to forgive and to transform. One important difference is that God's forgiveness is complete, while the divine work of transformation is always partial as long as we are still in this life. Baptism is God's promise to bring about forgiveness and transformation both in the present and future.

Luther's fresh insight in regard to baptism is to see its *ongoing, indeed, daily significance*. That is, acceptance and transformation need to be experienced again and again, and the physical symbolism of baptism can help us remember God's promise and experience God's merciful grace each day. If we take this important insight seriously, baptism can become a part of our everyday lives. This might seem strange, for many of us cannot even remember our baptism. And even those who can remember it find that the event of their baptism every year recedes further into the past. The point is not to recall the details of our baptismal ceremony—where it took place, what we wore, and so forth; rather, what counts is to call to mind the promised blessings of baptism: forgiveness and renewal through dying and rising with Christ. Baptism can be a powerful means of daily grace as we come to Christ frequently to receive acceptance and transformation.

The ongoing significance of baptism is rooted in Scripture where Paul says that those who have been baptized were baptized into Christ's death and resurrection (Romans 6:1-11). Martin Luther emphasizes that these two parts of baptism—the slaying of the old self and the rising of the new self—must continue all through life. "Thus a Christian life is nothing else than a daily baptism, once begun and ever continued." Where this amendment of life does not take place, Luther says baptism is being resisted. "Where faith is present with its fruits, there baptism is no empty symbol, but the effect accompanies it; but where faith is lacking, it remains a mere unfruitful sign."[7] Recent decades have seen a renewed stress in Lutheran circles on this ongoing, daily significance of baptism. While not unique to the Lutheran tradition, this emphasis on daily remembrance and living of baptism is certainly a prominent, common theme in Lutheran spirituality.

A question about baptism that is still hotly debated today is whether it is appropriate to baptize little children. Most churches, including the Lutheran, Eastern Orthodox, Roman Catholic, Reformed/Presbyterian,

Anglican/Episcopal, and Methodist, allow the baptism of small children as well as adults, whereas Baptist, Pentecostal, and Evangelical churches permit only baptism of those old enough to make their own confession of faith. The basic issue is the meaning of baptism. As I see it, the whole matter boils down to where people place the accent in their understanding of baptism.

On the one hand, those who reject infant baptism understand the sacrament as an outward declaration of a person's inward faith. Thus they insist that baptism is appropriate only when an individual has come to a personal faith in Christ and then wants to make a public confession of that faith in order to join the church. Baptism is like a new citizen taking an oath of allegiance to the nation. In this view, the accent falls on two factors: the individual's act of faith and the individual's decision to join the church.

On the other hand, those who accept baptism of infants as well as adults see baptism chiefly as an outward sign of God's grace that touches a person through the Christian message proclaimed and lived in the church. In this perspective, the accent falls on two different factors: God's grace and the church community within which the individual is nurtured.

In reality, the contrast between these two practices is not total, for each gives subordinate place to the factors stressed by the other. Those who practice only adult, or what they call believer, baptism generally acknowledge that God's grace precedes human faith, but they see that grace operating outside and before baptism. What they stress in baptism is the human response of faith to divine grace. In their view, baptism is not a means of grace. Those who reject infant baptism also recognize the importance of placing a child within the Christian community, for they frequently offer the option of a dedication ceremony in which parents dedicate their young children to God. Nevertheless, the believer baptism outlook mainly emphasizes the individual's act of faith and decision to join the church. In an era in which individualism has greatly increased in Western culture, this approach to baptism has seemed most reasonable to many people.

For their part, Lutherans and others who permit infant baptism give subordinate attention to the individual's response of faith and mature decision to identify with the church. A familiar corporate

expression of these concerns among Lutherans is the rite of Confirmation. Yet the primary emphasis of the Lutheran tradition in
respect to baptism is on the grace of God that is prior to the human
response of faith and on the formative influence of the Christian
community that invites the individual's mature commitment to
membership.

The main question believer baptism supporters ask about infant
baptism is this: How can a rite have any meaning for a person when
he or she doesn't understand what is happening? The best answer I
know is to compare baptism with adoption. In Western societies,
adoption generally has little or no pomp associated with it, for all
that is required is the signing of some documents. Yet adoption of a
young child is a momentous event, for it gives the child and the family a new lifelong relationship.

I know from personal experience that adoption is a helpful analogy for the understanding of baptism held by Lutherans. Our son Kim
had virtually nothing to say about his adoption at the age of four and
one-half years. Yet the adoption had a tremendous impact on his life,
for it transferred him from being an orphan in Korea to being a
member of the Hanson family in the United States. Belonging to the
Hanson family has created a web of mutually supportive relationships as well as immersion in white middle-class American language
and culture. Kim is still in the process of working out his own synthesis of Asian and American culture and establishing his own adult
relationships within the family.

What adoption illustrates is how an action taken quite apart from
a child's agreement is by no account a meaningless rite. Three points
stand out. First, my wife and I regard our decision to adopt Kim as
irrevocable. If someday Kim were to reject us, we would continue to
regard him as our son and hope for reconciliation with him. Similarly, in baptism God's promise of grace that forgives and transforms
always holds good. Even if a baptized person turns away from God,
God seeks reconciliation. God's promises given in baptism can be a
reminder of the merciful grace of God.[8]

Second, if Kim were to reject us as parents and persist in that rejection, our relationship with him would suffer alienation. Even though
we continue to love him and seek reconciliation, the alienation would

not be healed until he accepted us once again. In similar fashion, it is possible for someone baptized as a child to later turn away from God. While God's promises in baptism always hold good and God always seeks out the one who turns away, the broken relationship is not healed until God's love is accepted by the person.

Third, baptism, like adoption, is meant to signal ongoing involvement in a certain community. Just as the adopted child is intended to live within a family, so the baptized person is meant to live within the church where the Christian message is proclaimed. Thus before any child is baptized, there should be assurances that those responsible will have the child participate in a Christian community of worship.

Holy Communion

At the time of the Lutheran Reformation there was considerable controversy over what is variously called Holy Communion, the Lord's supper, or eucharist. One practice in the Roman Catholic Church to which Martin Luther objected was giving only the bread to laypeople; he insisted that everyone receive both bread and wine. This is no longer a point of contention, for in the late 1960s the Roman Catholic Church began to offer people both elements. An issue still discussed is in what sense the Lord's supper should be called a sacrifice; Lutherans fear that some uses of sacrificial language suggest that the Lord's supper is our offering to God rather than God's gift to us.

Controversies aside, Holy Communion, like Holy Baptism, is at the same time simple and profound. It is simple, for outwardly it is just the act of a community of Christians hearing some words that Jesus spoke at the Last Supper before his death and then eating some bread and drinking some wine. This joining of significant words with certain physical elements is a commonly recognized mark of a sacrament. Hearing the words alone or consuming bread and wine alone would not constitute Holy Communion. Yet the simple act of Holy Communion is so profound that even in a lifetime we never exhaust its rich meanings. Out of the wealth of meanings suggested in the New Testament and church tradition, we shall focus on three benefits from Holy Communion: communion with Christ, forgiveness, and strengthened faith.

1. The very name *Holy Communion* identifies this action as a special occasion for *communion with Christ.* Of course, it is also a time for communion with fellow Christians and, as the physical elements of bread and wine suggest, even communion with nature. Yet the heart of the Lord's supper experience is communion with Christ. *Communion* means a close sharing with another, and Holy Communion is an opportunity for intimate fellowship with Christ.

The foundation of this intimate fellowship is the presence of Christ himself. If Christ is far away, then there can be no intimate communion with him. Luther and the Lutheran tradition have affirmed the full presence of Christ through their teaching of the *real presence* of Christ in the Lord's supper. The Lutheran tradition holds that in these words, "This is my body . . . This is my blood," Jesus means what he says. In some way or other, Christ's body and blood are truly present. The Lutheran confessions do not claim to know *how* they are present, but their presence is real.

Why stress this apparently irrational belief? There are two points at stake. The first is that where we can be most confident of meeting the God of merciful grace is in the human being Jesus. If we rely upon our observations of nature and our own powers of reason, we are very likely to end up with a view of God as cool and aloof. But if we focus on God as revealed in Jesus and especially his cross, then we see a loving God who shares our suffering. Remember that this is the thrust of Luther's theology of the cross. Yet a dead or absent Jesus does us no good either; only a living and present Jesus can help. So the belief that Christ's body and blood are really present in the Lord's supper is a way of affirming that Jesus himself is somehow truly present here. To eat and to drink here is to take Christ into oneself.

The second and related point at stake in the real presence teaching is that it puts the main accent on divine grace, on Christ coming to us in the Lord's supper, rather than stressing that it is up to us to make Christ present in our memory. As with baptism, priority is given to God's grace, and the human responses of faith and memory are secondary. So real presence is drastically different from the widely held *memorial view,* which says the actions of eating bread and drinking wine are merely vivid ways of jogging our memory to recall what Jesus did long ago with his death. Lutheran teaching agrees that in the

Lord's supper Christians should call to mind the death of Jesus, yet they believe this memorial aspect is a subordinate theme.

The contrast between the real presence and memorial outlooks is clearly seen in the following manner. In the memorial view, when a person goes to Holy Communion, Christ is present only if the person remembers and thinks about Christ. Christ's presence is understood only *subjectively*; it is a presence only in the mind of the believer. If a person is thinking about something else during communion, Christ is not present to him or her. In the real presence view, Christ is truly present to each and every person who receives Holy Communion whether or not a person is thinking about Jesus, indeed, whether or not a person has faith in Christ. In this outlook, there is an *objective presence* of Christ. To be sure, only those with faith receive the benefits of Christ's objective presence, yet he is really present to all.

The Lutheran understanding of real presence is somewhat different from the Roman Catholic teaching of *transubstantiation,* although they share much in common. The chief difference is that Roman Catholic doctrine teaches that the substance or inner reality of the bread and wine actually become Christ's body and blood, so there is a permanent change that takes place. Consequently, when consecrated bread is not consumed at a eucharist, Roman Catholics reserve it in a special container called a tabernacle and many will show respect for this reserved body of Christ by kneeling as they enter church (genuflect). Lutherans believe that Christ's body and blood are present "in, with, and under" the bread and wine, but they think this presence lasts only for the duration of the Lord's supper. Nonetheless, Lutherans and Roman Catholics share a belief in the objective presence of Christ in the eucharist. Both say that one receives the body and blood of Christ in the eucharist. This belief in Christ's objective presence is not just idle speculation, but is the firm basis for experiencing Holy Communion as intimate communion with Christ.[9]

The manner of distributing Holy Communion varies. In Baptist, Evangelical, Pentecostal, and Reformed/Presbyterian churches, the usual procedure is for the bread and wine to be distributed to the congregation as they remain seated in their pews; when all has been distributed, then everyone eats and drinks at the same time. This procedure is strongly expressive of the communion of believers in Holy Communion. In a great many Lutheran churches, the custom is for people to come forward and kneel at the altar rail to receive communion. In some of these churches, this is the only time during the service that people kneel. Why do Lutherans often kneel when receiving communion? Kneeling is a bodily gesture that expresses deep reverence. I suggest that the reverential act of kneeling for communion is symbolic testimony to belief in the real presence of Christ.

2. Holy communion is closely linked with *divine acceptance* and the *forgiveness of sins,* because it is a reminder of Jesus' death and brings one into the presence of him who died for the sins of others. The New Testament has four somewhat varying accounts of Jesus' words at the Last Supper prior to his crucifixion, and all of them include some reference to these actions as indicative of Jesus' death for the sins of others. Martin Luther put the strongest emphasis on this meaning. For example, in his Small Catechism he says the benefit of this eating and drinking is "forgiveness of sins, life, and salvation," and he does not explain what "life and salvation" add to forgiveness.[10]

For most Lutherans, forgiveness has probably been the central meaning of the Lord's supper. Especially after the practice of private confession had largely died out among Lutherans by the 1700s, they have turned to Holy Communion for special assurance of forgiveness. This is somewhat unfortunate, for it narrows the range of experience people have of the sacrament. It also tends to make the eucharist a somber time in which the many celebratory elements of the eucharist are overlooked. Nevertheless, forgiveness is one of the important meanings of Holy Communion.

3. The Lord's supper also *strengthens faith.* The name *Lord's supper* suggests that it is an occasion for receiving nourishment. The need for repeated nourishment comes from the fact that in this life our faith is never perfect. Remember that while part of faith is believing certain things to be true, the heart of faith is trusting in God or Christ. As we saw in chapter 3, the fundamental aspect of the Christian life is to live with confidence in the merciful grace of God in all situations. As we well know from experience, this is by no means easy.

Time and again, we find ourselves trusting more in ourselves or some human scheme than in God. So living as a Christian is a continual struggle between our desire to trust in God/Christ and our tendency to rely primarily upon human resources. The Lord's supper strengthens faith by again bringing the believer into intimate communion with the transforming power of Christ.

As we look back over these three meanings, we can see that the Lord's supper reinforces the believer's relationship with God articulated in the doctrine of justification by grace through faith. We recall that according to the doctrine of justification, God's grace includes both assurance of complete acceptance and forgiveness and partial transformation to a renewed life of faith and love. As a basic means of grace, the Lord's supper bestows both forms of grace: acceptance/forgiveness and strengthened faith. This grace is found in communion with Christ, and the physical, symbolic actions of the Lord's supper reinforce the closeness of that communion.

CONFESSION AND ABSOLUTION

In his Large Catechism, Martin Luther says confession is what we do, while absolution is what God does. He recognizes that there are different forms of confession of sin: to God alone, to another person with whom there is enmity, before others in public, and privately to a third party from whom one seeks advice, comfort, and strength. Absolution is the work God does in forgiving one's sin through the word spoken by another person. Both confession and absolution are vital, but absolution is what we should concentrate on.[11] This strong endorsement of confession and absolution is fully consistent with the Lutheran emphasis on the merciful grace of God. Since the primary Lutheran accent falls on the forgiving mercy of God, the announcement of this forgiveness in absolution is crucial.

What has been most consistently done among Lutherans is *public* confession and absolution, for that is commonly the first part of the worship service. Even though usually it was not called a sacrament, *private* confession and absolution continued to be practiced in many Lutheran areas for about two centuries before it largely died out. The key feature of both practices is that the one who confesses hears the message of God's forgiveness in Christ spoken by another person.

Why not just confess to God alone and believe in one's heart that God forgives? Of course, we appropriately do this in our personal daily prayers. But if that is all we do, if we never confess our sin to another person and never hear someone else announce the gospel of God's grace, then we run into difficulty. The difficulty is that we readily become trapped in our own imagination, for we tend to create our own version of divine forgiveness and our own picture of God. We miss out on the healing power of God. This is mainly why Luther says it is crucial to stay close to God's "external word," that is, the gospel of God's grace that comes from outside ourselves.[12] As we have noted, Luther says this gospel comes to us through absolution as well as through proclamation, baptism, and the Lord's supper. This external word has the power to create a new relationship with God and other people that takes us beyond the possibilities within our own power. So when we confess our sin and hear the words of absolution announced by another person, we should treasure those words as God's own message to us.

In reality, though, it is common to go through a public rite of confession and absolution without being mindful of the possibilities. Private confession and absolution can be another channel for God's grace to work in our lives. Confession with one other person enables us to acknowledge our specific sins, to bring them out of the darkness of our memory into the light. Having done so, that person's announcement of God's grace of forgiveness and renewal is more likely to be heard as God's own healing word. Luther says private confession is not commanded by God. Yet there is no doubt that Luther and the Lutheran confessions strongly encourage use of a rite of private confession such as those available in some contemporary Lutheran service books.[13]

It's clear that in the Lutheran confessional writings confession and absolution is a very important means of grace. Although Lutherans do not ordinarily call it a sacrament, it is a rite in which God addresses people through words.

SACRAMENTS AND SACRAMENTALITY

Imagine that we take a tour of churches from various Christian traditions and begin with an Orthodox church. The inside of the church is rich in images called icons and other visual symbols; the garments of the priest during the worship service are ornate. Many people purchase a candle and light it while kneeling to pray before an icon that they also sometimes touch. At times during the worship service, incense involves one's nose in the action. When the words of the liturgy and complex musical responses of the choir are added, the worship experience here seems to touch all one's senses. As we talk with a priest afterward, we find that the Orthodox church has eucharist every Sunday and they believe that the bread and wine become the body and blood of Christ.

Next our tour takes us to a Baptist church. The interior of the church is quite plain with little visual symbolism other than a cross. To one side is a small empty pool for baptisms by immersion. The most prominent object at the front of the church is the pulpit from which the minister in plain black robe leads the worship and delivers a rather lengthy, spirited sermon. A strong organ leads the congregation in singing lively hymns, and a large robed choir sings a heartfelt anthem. In speaking with the minister later, we learn that this Baptist church has Holy Communion six times a year and believes it is a memorial to remind people of Christ's sacrifice. The overall impression of this experience is that hearing is the primary means of communication in this church, although the rhythm and warmth of the music involve the body. The senses of sight, smell, and touch are not much engaged.

As our tour of other churches proceeds, we begin to see a pattern that reminds us of the chart of church traditions on page 13:

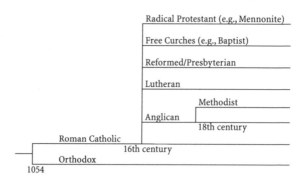

Those churches at the bottom of the chart—the Orthodox church and Roman Catholic Church—teach that in the eucharist people receive the body and blood of Christ, celebrate the eucharist every Sunday, and generally have church buildings rich in various forms of physical symbols. They also recognize seven sacraments and tend to regard sacraments, rather than words, as the primary means by which God communicates grace. Those churches at the top of the chart—Mennonite, Baptist, Evangelical, Pentecostal—teach that the eucharist is a memorial of Christ's death, generally celebrate the eucharist rather infrequently, and usually have church buildings with few physical symbols. These churches also recognize just two sacraments and clearly see word as the primary way that God meets them.

In short, I think there is a correlation between, on the one hand, the understanding and practice of the eucharist and other sacraments and, on the other hand, the prominence given nonverbal symbols. Those traditions that stress sacraments in their worship life and hold a "realistic" understanding of Christ's presence in the eucharist also place high value on other physical symbols. Those traditions that give minimal attention to sacraments and teach the more cerebral memorial view of Christ's presence tend to have few other physical symbols. This correlation should not surprise us, for the Lord's supper and other sacraments involve the use of physical symbols and bodily actions. It is reasonable that the attitude taken toward the nonverbal symbolism of sacraments will be reflected in the stance toward nonverbal symbolism generally. This broader appreciation for nonverbal symbolism as means of divine communication is often called *sacramentality*. Some church traditions have a high degree of sacramentality, other traditions a low degree of it.

Among churches, Lutherans occupy a middle ground in respect to sacraments and sacramentality. While Lutherans have regarded words as the chief means through which God communicates with us, they have varied greatly in the prominence they have given to sacraments and nonverbal symbols. In history and today there have been Lutherans churches that have Holy Communion just four times a year and whose sanctuaries are devoid of visual symbols except for a cross and a few candles. There have also been Lutheran churches that celebrate the Lord's supper weekly, have periodic remembrances of baptism using water, and whose worship services and church interiors are quite rich in nonverbal symbolism, even incense on occasion. And there are Lutheran churches that fall all along the spectrum between these poles. In recent years, among many Lutherans there has been a movement toward more frequent communion and a renewed emphasis on the continuing significance of baptism. Still, there is often a lack of appreciation for nonverbal symbolism. For example, frequently a stress on the daily meaning of baptism takes the form of merely recalling the significance of baptism. The process is strictly mental and limited to thinking with words about baptism. Yet some Lutheran churches reinforce remembrance of baptism with nonverbal symbolism such as dipping one's hand into water and making the sign of the cross on oneself; this, I suggest, is a more powerful form of remembrance.

Another variable in the picture is the culture of a people. When I observed Lutheran worship services of Hispanic and African American communities, they had more bodily involvement than northern European communities. The Hispanic and African American Lutherans moved more in rhythm with the music, which also had more of a beat, and they were more likely to hug and hold hands at times during the service. On the other hand, I have not seen more visual symbolism among Hispanic, African American, and African Lutherans. In fact, I was told by some Tanzanians that traditional East African culture did not emphasize visual symbolism; music was more highly valued than visual art. The point is that in addition to the middle ground stance of the Lutheran tradition toward nonverbal symbols, the culture of a people will also influence the weight given to such symbols.

The picture is complex for there are multiple influences. One will find a congregation of charismatic northern European Lutherans bodily involved in singing, praying with hands held high, embracing, and praying for physical healing. Here the charismatic subculture enters (e.g., the frequent use of *just* in prayers: "Lord, we just ask that you heal Sarah . . .). Nevertheless, the charismatic Pentecostal tradition gives little significance to sacraments and visual symbols. Thus the prominence given to nonverbal symbols in a particular community of

Lutherans results from the flowing together of several influences: the Lutheran tradition with its own variability, the traditional culture of the people, and other religious and cultural streams.

It's not that there is just one way that we must follow in respect to sacramental practice and sacramentality. It's more a matter of range and depth of communication. There is no doubt that words have the power to convey the Christian message whether the words be written, spoken, or sung. But we know from our experience that physical objects and bodily gestures are also very powerful means of communication. A picture, stained-glass window, or statue speak to us on another level. Laying on of hands adds something to a prayer expressed in words. Kneeling brings another dimension to the act of praying. A genuine hug adds warmth to a verbal peace.

The question is whether we in the Lutheran church have sufficiently tapped the rich resources on sacraments and sacramentality available in our own tradition and from other Christian traditions through ecumenical contacts. It is surely a matter worthy of thought, discussion, and experimentation. Rather than accept without thought all our current practices with sacraments and other physical symbols, it would be wise to reflect afresh on the issues.[14]

For Reflection and Practice

1. What has been the significance of baptism for you? Be honest as you reflect upon your own experience. Try to refrain from merely repeating a textbook answer. If you are in a group, after several minutes of individual reflection, join together with two or three others to share your thoughts.

2. Here are some ways of using water to strengthen mindfulness of the grace of baptism:

a. When you wash your face in the morning, let the water remind you of God's grace in baptism.

b. Your congregation might place a bowl of water on a stand near entrances to the sanctuary. It might be suggested that people dip their hand into the water and make the sign of the cross as at their baptism. As slaves were once marked, so Christians at baptism are marked to show to whom they belong. Some instruction on making the sign of the cross might be appreciated: touch forehead, then middle chest, upper left side of chest, and upper right side of chest. When I do this entering church, I think of God's mercy, acceptance with generous forgiveness. When I do it leaving church, I think of God's grace that will continue to transform my life.

c. Some churches place their open baptismal font with water in a position so that people pass it on their way to communion and may dip their hand into the water.

d. At a baptism or during the creed at the Easter Vigil, the pastor may use an evergreen bough to sprinkle water on members of the congregation to aid them in affirming their baptism anew.

e. Following the practice of the ancient church, use the Lenten season for catechetical study in preparation for baptism or reaffirmation of baptism at the Easter Vigil.

3. Reflect on your congregation's practice of Holy Communion. What are the reasons for the frequency of communion in your church? What are the reasons your church distributes communion in the way it does? Be honest. Are these sound reasons? Do you think there should be any changes? Why? These questions can be used for either individual reflection or group discussion.

4. What has Holy Communion, in fact, meant for you at different stages in your life? To what extent is participation in Holy Communion a regular practice for you? How might your communion with Christ be deepened further through the Lord's supper?

5. In addition to the regular practice of public confession and absolution in Lutheran worship, there is the rite of Individual Confession and Forgiveness in the Evangelical Lutheran Church of America (ELCA) *Lutheran Book of Worship*, pp. 196–97, and The Lutheran Church—Missouri Synod *Lutheran Worship*, pp. 310–11. Remember that pastor and penitent are free to adapt such a rite to their circumstances. Read through the rite once, and then go through it again step-by-step, putting yourself in the place of the penitent. The words there are spoken to you and by you. The sins confessed are your sins. Take your time and think about what you are doing. Afterward, either alone or together with others, reflect back on the experience.

6. Examine the exterior of your church building and its sanctuary for visual symbolism. Is there symbolism built into the very structure of the building? What symbols do you find in the sanctuary? What symbols are permanent? Changing? If you are in a group, the whole body may first break down into individuals or small numbers to examine the church and then come all together to compare findings.

7. What role do other physical objects and bodily gestures play in your congregation's worship? Some possibilities: receiving ashes on Ash Wednesday, stripping of the altar on Maundy Thursday, adoring a rough-hewn cross on Good Friday, laying on of hands in various contexts, anointing for healing, coming forward to the altar, standing, kneeling, making the sign of the cross, shaking hands during the peace, hugging during the peace, forming a prayer circle and holding hands, swaying to the music, dancing, clapping, leaving after the service (do people mill about as they depart or are they ushered out by rows?), gathering before or after for conversation and coffee. How does culture influence the use of physical objects and bodily gestures in worship? These questions are suitable for either private reflection or group discussion. If your group is rather large, it would be best to first have smaller clusters discuss the questions before coming all together.

6

CHRISTIAN SPIRITUALITY AND THE CHURCH

ATTITUDES TOWARD THE CHURCH'S ROLE in religious or spiritual life vary tremendously. In respect to church membership, some sociological studies divide people into three categories: loyalists, the unaffiliated, and returners. To these we should add a fourth category: first-time joiners. *Loyalists* are those who consistently identify themselves with a church. In his study of baby boomers (those born between 1946 and 1964), Wade Clark Roof found that one-third of them fell into this category. Those who are *unaffiliated* have either grown up unchurched or have dropped out of church; in either case, at the time of being surveyed they were not connected with a church or other religious institution. Disengagement from any institutional religion is common in America; some research indicates that about one-half of Americans drop out of organized religion for at least two years sometime during their lifetime. *Returners* are those who have dropped out of church and then come back. Sometimes the period of disengagement from church lasts a long time. *First-time joiners* are people who grew up without any attachment to a church and then enter one.

A recent sociological study shows that family bonds are the most important *social* factor influencing church affiliation. Three family bonds are especially significant: relationship with parent(s), marriage, and children. That is, those persons who have a close relationship with their parents are more likely to belong to a church than those who are distant. Those who are married are more apt to be a church member than the unmarried. Having a child also makes church affiliation more probable. Overall, those individuals who are personally distant from parents, unmarried, and childless are least likely to be affiliated with a church.[1]

A study of baby boomers confirmed that family is the most frequently cited reason for returning to the church, but as additional reasons it also reported a personal quest for meaning and the importance of belonging to a community of faith.[2] It appears that the personal quest for meaning becomes increasingly influential as people grow older. When asked whether many baby boomers were returning to the church, pollster George Gallup Jr. said, "Yes. It's inevitable. As they're getting older and encountering mortality, they're coming back to the church."[3] In other words, affiliation and nonaffiliation with a religious institution are linked in complex ways with a person's own faith development.

FAITH DEVELOPMENT

Faith development has been the topic of considerable research in recent years. The foremost scholar in this area is James Fowler, who distinguishes seven stages of faith. It is important to note that Fowler says these stages may be observed in persons of different faiths—religious faiths such as Christianity or Hinduism as well as secular faiths such as communism or egoism. A classic example of egoistic faith comes from Ayn Rand in her book *The Virtue of Selfishness,* which attacked altruism and exalted concern with one's own interests.[4] So James Fowler's stages of faith do not refer to the content of a person's faith, but the manner in which the person holds it. Three of his stages are especially relevant for our discussion.[5]

Stage 4: Synthetic-Conventional Faith. A person with a synthetic-conventional faith has drawn together various stories, beliefs, and values into a personal synthesis, yet it is called a conventional faith since its elements are drawn from significant others such as family and peers. For instance, a young woman from a family committed to Ayn Rand's egoism might sift through the beliefs and values of family members, school friends, and her favorite rock musicians and television shows to formulate her own version of an egoistic faith.

Or a teenage boy from a Christian family might pull together his own understanding of the Christian faith that he sees in his family, close friends, congregation, and local community. A synthetic-conventional faith is not a child's faith, for here the individual has thought through the faith of his or her significant community and formed a personal version of it. For instance, an older child in a Christian context will generally understand the seven-day creation story of Genesis 1 in a literal way. A Christian in the fourth stage might well interpret this creation story as meaning seven long periods of time; this is how the person synthesizes the biblical story and what is taught in middle school or high school science. Yet a fourth-stage faith is conventional, for the individual has not yet stood outside that faith and examined it critically. People commonly form a synthetic-conventional faith during their teens and may persist in it into their forties and perhaps for life.

Stage 5: Individuative-Reflective Faith. Events may lead one to question one's synthetic-conventional faith. Leaving home does this for many young adults; going away to work, entering the military, or going away to college often does it. Leaving home and entering into a different social context may prompt one to see one's faith from the outside, as it were. Confronted by different beliefs and values, one frequently looks at one's faith with a more critical eye. This may simply prompt a person to adopt another conventional faith with a different group. For instance, going to college and adopting the outlook and values of a fraternity or sorority might be replacing one conventional faith for another. However, encountering a different social context also may lead to the fifth stage of faith in Fowler's conception. For adults in their thirties or forties, transition to the fifth stage can be precipitated by changes in primary relationships, such as a divorce or death of a loved one.

Fowler says two closely related things must happen in order to arrive at an individuative-reflective faith. One is that a person takes on more responsibility for his or her life. Whereas someone in stage 4 is immersed in his or her social relationships, now one becomes more independent. It's possible that one may continue to live in the same social context, but now a person gains a sense of one's own self behind the various roles one plays. So a more independent self must emerge. The other thing that must happen is critical reflection on faith that results in a person choosing his or her beliefs and commitments. Here one's independence is applied to a person's faith.

Going through the transition from one faith stage to another is generally difficult, and this is certainly true of moving from stage 4 to 5. One often feels as though one's world has been turned upside down. One experiences disorientation, anxiety, struggle. There is frequently a powerful encounter with the cultural relativity of convictions and lifestyles. There may seem to be no universal truth or right. The transition is extended in time, often lasting five to seven years or longer. Fowler says this transition is usually less severe when it happens in young adulthood, but more difficult in the late thirties or early forties when it impacts a more established system of relationships.[6]

The faith that emerges in stage 5 has various gains and losses. Among the gains of an individuative-reflective faith are that it is more aware of other faiths, it is more explicit, and it is more self-conscious about what rituals and symbols mean. This attention to what symbols mean involves both gain and loss. For example, a Christian with a fifth-stage faith might abandon the attempt to reconcile the seven days of Genesis 1 with evolution by the former method of extending the duration of the days, and now simply say the biblical account is an imaginative way of teaching certain basic truths about God, the world, and human beings. This is a gain in that it makes for greater intellectual coherence. It is a loss in the fact that it tends to flatten out the rich meanings of symbols into what can be clearly stated.

Sometimes this flattening goes so far as to reduce rich symbols to something else. For instance, theologian Harvey Cox once told how, as an eighteen-year-old, he attended mass with his Catholic girlfriend who had just taken a college anthropology course. As people were receiving the eucharist, she whispered to him, "'That's just a primitive totemic ritual, you know.' Harvey said, 'A what?' She replied with great self-assurance, 'A primitive totemic ritual. Almost all premodern religious and tribal groups have them. They are ceremonies where worshipers bind themselves together and to the power of the sacred by a cannibalistic act of ingesting the manna of a dead god.'"[7] Here the rich symbolism of a religious ritual is reduced to what appears to be an analytical fact, and the person making the analysis seems superior to those who are engaged by the ritual.

Stage 6: Conjunctive Faith. Many who arrive at a stage 5 faith never leave it, but others experience difficulties with it and make a transition to what Fowler calls "conjunctive faith." Fowler says conjunctive faith is unusual before midlife, which he says begins at about age thirty-five, although I have observed conjunctive faith in a twenty-year-old who had been coping for quite a few years with several serious health conditions. The term *conjunctive faith* suggests bringing together different things, as does a linguistic conjunction (for example: and, or, but). Conjunctive faith brings together and accepts the polarities and paradoxes present in ourselves, in society, and in Ultimate Reality. A person becomes more aware of polar forces in one's own existence such as conscious-unconscious and good-evil. The realities of middle age may lead one to face personal limitations and unfulfilled dreams. Involvement with loss and suffering often precipitates a crisis of faith. One's understanding of God or Ultimate Reality no longer fits with experience. Truth is felt to be more complex than previously thought. The above anthropology student's excessive confidence in having grasped the full truth frequently appears inadequate as life proceeds. Accordingly, one who makes this transition comes to sense that symbol and ritual cannot be adequately reduced to neat mental categories; a new appreciation for rich symbolism arises. Furthermore, conjunctive faith has a genuine openness to the truths of traditions other than one's own, while not succumbing to relativism in which the quest for truth is abandoned in a sea of different opinions. Fowler says, "Conjunctive faith exhibits a combination of committed belief in and through the particularities of a tradition, while insisting upon the humility that knows that the grasp on ultimate truth that any of our traditions can offer needs continual correction and challenge. This is to help overcome blind spots (blind *sides*) as well as the tendencies to idolatry . . . to which all of our traditions are prone."[8]

Transition from one stage of faith to another frequently involves confusion and struggle that can stretch over a number of years. During the move from stage 3 to 4, which often occurs in early adolescence, Fowler has interviewed a number of what he calls "eleven-year-old atheists." These young people experienced conflicts with their previously held conception that in day-to-day existence God rewarded the good and punished the wicked. Since this idea of God no longer fit their experience, they concluded that God did not exist, or as one girl put it, is asleep. The transition from stage 4 to 5 is generally precipitated by major changes in the primary human relationships in the person's life—moving away from home, a divorce. The shift from stage 5 to 6 is initiated sometimes by traumatic events such as divorce or death, other times by inner trials such as midlife crisis. For some people, these transitions happen relatively smoothly, but for many—and especially those who have suffered a great loss—the passage is very stressful and stormy.

Factors Contributing to Alienation from Church

For teenage or adult persons going through a transition from one stage of faith to another, it is quite common to withdraw from a previous faith community and either join another community or float without group attachment. Not that every adult who goes through such a transition drops out of church or other religious group, for people consistently loyal to the church also develop their faith. Nonetheless, a transition in faith often results in a church member dropping out. No doubt many factors are involved in whether a person continues in church without significant interruption, drops out for a while and returns, or remains unaffiliated. We have already noted some factors: quality of relationship with parents, marriage, and children. One could also reasonably add the nature of the parents' faith; a parent with deep Christian faith and close church ties is more likely to have adult children attached to the church than is a parent with merely a nominal faith and church connection.

Another major factor that contributes to dropping out of church is the church's failure. Some persons who have experience with a church have been hurt or disappointed by it. Whether it be mainly an individual's relationship with his or her family, congregation, or large church institution, church can be experienced negatively in various ways. In some cases, in spite of a church's official theology, what a

person feels with church are not mercy and love but mostly require-
ments and demands. In other cases, although church banners may
proclaim loving service to others, what an individual actually sees are
struggles for power and bitter fights. Or persons may experience
exclusion and rejection in church; women or those not belonging to
the dominant group feel left out. Their point of view and needs are
persistently not represented. In short, another reason why people are
alienated from the church is that they have been hurt rather than
helped and spiritually starved rather than nourished by the church.

Another factor that works toward distance between individuals
and church in Western societies, and especially the United States, is
that our culture not only stresses independence of the individual but
also currently includes a widespread distrust of almost all social institutions. In an age when there is deep suspicion of government,
schools, the legal system, health care, marriage, and family, it is highly
unlikely that the church would be exempt. Some of us who have
grown up in this culture may view this suspicion as normal, but it is
very different from many other cultures in the world. In any event,
such cultural attitudes reinforce the conviction that individuals do
not really need a community of faith.

Yet another factor that adds to alienation from church may be an
excessive sense of self-sufficiency. This is not surprising, for a fundamental ingredient of sin is trust in human resources rather than in
God. Everyone has to contend with this sinful self-sufficiency, including the most loyal church member. With all of us there is a tendency
to believe that we can manage life satisfactorily without constant
reliance on God. However, with non-churchgoers this exaggerated
self-sufficiency may fortify a belief that they can be good Christians
without regular involvement with the word of God or reception of
the eucharist.

Excessive self-sufficiency is not new. In fact, we behave in ways
quite similar to the ancient Israelites in the Old Testament. A persistent theme in the Old Testament prophets is criticism of the widespread Israelite practice of offering sacrifices to Ba'al and Asheroth at
numerous shrines around the country. While on the surface this may
seem crude to us, in reality the Israelites were simply hedging their
bets. Their God, Yahweh, was associated with the nomadic way of life

that the Israelites had known before settling down to pursue agriculture in the promised land. Ba'al and Asheroth were associated with fertility in agriculture. Many Israelites wanted to make sure they would get good crops by also making offerings to Ba'al. They didn't think they were rejecting Yahweh, but it seemed too risky to bet everything on the God of Israel. So they hedged their bets by putting something down, so to speak, on both Yahweh and the fertility deities Ba'al and Asheroth.

The temptation is to do much the same today. Not that we think of offering something before statues of Ba'al and Asheroth, but there are many ways of religiously hedging our bets. For instance, instead of relying centrally on Jesus Christ made known in the word of God and sacraments, it is tempting to fashion our own conception of God from a multitude of sources, including popular culture, self-help schemes, psychological theories, and sacred texts from various religions. There is a subtle but crucial difference between a humble quest for wisdom about God from various traditions and an I'm-in-the-driver's-seat management of spiritual and religious sources. Often what is going on is that we are spreading our bets, dividing our loyalties, as we think best. We may be very religious or deeply spiritual, but it is religion or spirituality on our terms. Excessive self-sufficiency is at work.

When we add to these factors that our society is highly mobile, rapidly changing, and very pluralistic, it is not surprising that many people who have had some connection with a church drop out— some permanently, others for a period of varying duration.

Our Own Experience of Church

The fact is that experience with the church is highly variable. A good way to reflect on our own feelings about church is to take an honest look at our past experience with the church. The following exercise will help you do this. Take a standard-sized sheet of unlined paper, place it so the longer side is horizontal in front of you, and draw a line in the middle from left to right. This line represents your lifeline up to this point, so your birth is at the far left end and today at the far right. Divide the line into ten- and five-year time units, perhaps adding shorter lines for single years, like this:

Now on the top side of the horizontal line, start with your earliest years and make notations understandable to you of any positive memories you have of church. Remember that church is not limited to that community gathered for worship or Sunday school, but is also Christians dispersed in families and daily activities of life. For the moment, set aside any bad memories of church, and let positive memories surface—persons, groups, events. Gently call them to mind without trying to analyze or criticize them. If you have many memories, just note a few and then move on to the next block of time in your life until you reach the present. Then on the bottom side of the horizontal line, go through from your childhood onward and note any negative memories you have of church. Again resist analyzing or evaluating these memories; simply notice them and pass on to the next time period.

When you have finished, look back over your sheet to see any significant patterns. What persons have been the strongest influences on your attitude toward church? Has church had different significance for you at different points in your life? Are those shifts in your relationship with church correlated with other major events in your life such as adolescent rebellion, leaving home, marriage, divorce, birth of a child, death of a loved one, serious illness? Are those shifts related to events in your church such as a conflict, something the pastor did, or a change in leadership? On balance, has your experience of church been positive or negative?

What Do We Mean by *Church?*

Recently I asked a class of college students this question, "If a person wants to be a good Christian, how important is it to participate in church?" I asked them to express their answer in terms of a number between zero and ten. Zero would mean participation in church is not important at all and ten would mean it is extremely important. I received answers ranging from three to ten. The ensuing discussion revealed that answers depended greatly on what the students meant by *church*.

For many, *church* meant "going to church." That is, church was equated with what happens on Sunday mornings when a certain group of people gather in a church building for Christian worship. Those who understood church in this sense tended to give a lower number in answer to the question. For a few people, *church* meant being physically together with other Christians whether in worship or a business meeting. Since these persons said they found more spiritual growth through solitude and private meditation, they also answered with a low score. For a few others, *church* was closely identified with an organization with certain authoritative leaders. If they saw this organizational structure as a positive, they answered with a high number; if they saw the organization as a negative, they responded with a low number. For still others, *church* meant "Christian community," whether gathered in a church building for worship or singing around a campfire or remembering one another in private prayer even though separated by many miles. Those who understood church in this sense generally gave an answer with a high number. So the importance we see in church participation depends greatly on what we mean by *church*.

In this regard the understanding of church in the Lutheran tradition is instructive. The Lutheran confessions stress two points about the church.

1. Lutheran theology says *the church is the community of believers among whom the word of God is proclaimed and the sacraments rightly administered.*[9] This simple but fundamental statement needs some explanation.

   a. Notice that the church is understood primarily as the community of believers. This is different from those traditions that emphasize a certain organizational structure for the church. For instance, the Episcopal church regards bishops as essential (the term *Episcopal* comes from a Greek word for bishop) and the Roman Catholic Church insists on the office of the pope (the bishop of

Rome) as vital for the church. The Lutheran confessions stress that the church is first and foremost the whole community of people who believe in Jesus Christ. So the church should not be identified with a pastor, bishop, or some authoritative body, but should include all Christian believers whether gathered together for worship on Sunday or dispersed throughout the week. In other words, contrary to how we commonly use the word, *church* in the Lutheran tradition is not primarily understood as a social institution with a certain organization. Neither is *church* identified with a church building nor simply with what happens on Sunday morning in that building, "going to church." Rather, church is a community of believers in Christ. Surely, this community gathers for worship and study on Sunday mornings, but it is also church while members of the community are separated from one another and engaged in their daily activities. So one may encounter members of the church in one's family, at work, at school, or in a special interest group such as a Twelve Step group. Church is a community of believers in Christ both when gathered for worship and when dispersed in daily life.

While the church is primarily a community of people, it is also secondarily an organization with a structure. No human community can exist for long without adopting some sort of organization. So St. Luke's Lutheran Church in Erie, Pennsylvania, will have regular worship services, a pastor, church council, and certain committees, and be part of the larger structure of the Evangelical Lutheran Church in America. The Evangelical Lutheran Church in America is organized into synods, each of which coordinates and supervises the congregations in a region. Each synod has a bishop and makes major decisions in a synod assembly, which includes both lay and clergy representatives from the congregations. At the churchwide level, the ELCA makes big policy decisions in a churchwide assembly of lay and clergy delegates and directs national and worldwide activities through a presiding bishop and church council, and a number of administrative units. Other Lutheran churches around the world are organized in similar fashion, although the terminology may differ. For instance, in some Lutheran churches the regional unit is called a district or diocese and the title "district president" is used instead of "bishop." For Lutherans it is important to remember that church organization is intended to serve the gospel; if it fails to do so, it should be reformed.

b. In a world where there are many religious groups, how can we know where the church is? The Lutheran confessions answer by pointing out two marks of the church community: proclamation of the word of God and administration of the sacraments. Why focus on these two activities? Because Word and Sacrament are the principal means by which faith in Jesus Christ is created. There is confidence that wherever the word of God is proclaimed and the sacraments administered, some people will have faith in Jesus Christ. Thus there is a chicken-and-egg relation between the church, on the one hand, and Word and Sacrament, on the other hand. Word and Sacrament are the egg from which the church arises, while the church is the hen that lays the egg by proclaiming the word and administering the sacraments. Carrying out these tasks is the essential purpose of the church. This does not mean, however, that church is equated with "going to church." While the sacraments are ordinarily administered only at a worship service, the word is proclaimed not only on Sunday morning but also in a multitude of ways throughout the week. This leads us to our second point.

2. The second point in a Lutheran view of the church is that *although normally only ordained ministers publicly proclaim the word and administer the sacraments, all Christian believers are called by God to minister to others.* When it comes to *public* preaching and administration of sacraments, Lutherans have said these activities should ordinarily be done by someone duly appointed by the Christian community, namely, an ordained minister. This is for the sake of good order in the church community. In extraordinary circumstances, say when people are marooned, they might elect one of their number to preach, baptize, and administer communion for corporate worship, but in normal circumstances these key functions of public worship should be performed by an ordained minister.

A revolutionary part of Martin Luther's teaching was the *priesthood of all believers.* Unfortunately, this idea is very often misinterpreted as meaning merely that every individual has the right to bring his or her own needs directly to God without going through a priest as intermediary. In other words, it is commonly taken to mean "I am my own priest." Although it's true that a person may come directly to God to ask for forgiveness, that is not the thrust of Luther's idea of the priesthood of all believers. In his view, priests do not act for themselves but on behalf of others. Luther says, "As priests we are worthy to appear before God to pray for others and to teach one another divine things."[10] All Christians are called to minister to others not only in the general sense of serving others in daily life, but also in the specifically religious sense of praying for them and teaching them by life and speech about their merciful God. For instance, the priesthood of all believers succeeds when a believer who has been wronged by another shows that person forgiveness, when parents lead their children in prayer, when a person says to a friend, "I'll pray for you," or when Christians acknowledge their faith in a Twelve Step group. In the previous chapter, we noted another important way this mutual ministry of all believers is manifest: "the mutual conversation and consolation of the brothers [and sisters]." Whether done formally or informally, in the process of dealing with one another's sins and conflicts, members of the church bring about repentance and forgiveness.

The overall thrust of a Lutheran understanding of church is as a community of believers in Jesus Christ, a community created and sustained throughout the week as well as on Sunday by a broadly shared mutual ministry of word, sacrament, and prayer.

LITTLE STORY, BIG STORY

Our personal journeys involve us necessarily in a search for meaning. We are in the process of composing the little story of our lives with their unique series of events and concrete relationships; this is what we live from day to day. Yet we look for fuller meaning by connecting the little story of our lives with a Big Story, which sets forth a view of reality and the wider significance of human life.[11]

There are a considerable number of Big Stories. Many of them are religious, but some are secular. In this book we have been concerned with the Christian story. This story begins with God's creation of the world and an account of evil entering the world. It proceeds with

God's call to Abraham and Sarah, and establishment of a covenant with Israel. It continues with Israel's decline into slavery, exodus to the promised land, and all the ups and downs of its covenant relationship with God. The story reaches its high point in the life, death, and resurrection of Jesus followed by the spread of the Christian church and its message. And the story looks forward to its conclusion and fulfillment when God entirely overcomes all the powers of death and evil.

The church remains the primary carrier of the Christian Big Story. The church has written down that story in the Bible, sung it in music, enacted it in rituals, and portrayed it in Christian art. Even when an individual finds tremendous renewal in Christian faith through solitude and private meditation, that individual is still connected with the church through its scriptures and art, and in memory of its songs and rituals. Yet without a living community of Christians to proclaim and celebrate that Big Story, it would soon become a museum piece like Greek mythology. If a person is going to seriously engage the Christian story, then one will need to connect with the Christian community in some ongoing way.

For instance, if I wanted to shape my life by the Big Story of Zen Buddhism, I could accomplish something by reading some Buddhist scriptures, consulting other books on Buddhism, and watching videos. But if I want to get beyond merely scratching the surface, I will need to participate with some consistency in a Zen community where people experienced in that tradition can help me learn how to meditate and understand things in a Zen way. The situation would be somewhat different if I had grown up and lived in a Zen culture, for then some of the Zen story and practice would be in my memory. Nevertheless, those would be memories of my childhood and youth, and would not be adequate to the concerns and questions of an adult. To fashion an adult Buddhist faith, I would need to participate in a Buddhist community and learn as an adult.

Something very much like this, I suggest, is true for those who would live according to the Christian Big Story. I believe the hunger for meaning in life is always with us, although it may not be noticeable at times in our lives. When we feel secure, it's easy to put off paying attention to that hunger. Besides, the meaning found in the round of daily life and work may seem enough. But often when the security of life is shaken in some way, we begin to look for something deeper. This may lead us back to the church or, for someone who has been in the church all along, it may prompt a search on another level. As George Gallup Jr. said, when persons grow older and begin to face mortality, they are more likely to seek assistance from religious institutions in working out their personal answer to the question of meaning in life. Having the little story of our lives grounded in and shaped increasingly by the Christian Big Story is a lifelong enterprise.

The church as Christian community has at least three vital roles in shaping and nurturing Christian faith.

1. *Give instruction in Christian faith and practices.* No one is born with Christian faith or any other kind of faith. The Lutheran confessions teach both that faith in Christ is a divine gift, a fruit of the Holy Spirit's work in people's lives, and that the Spirit always makes use of natural means such as human beings and their words. So while faith is a divine gift, it is also true that in some sense we learn Christian faith. Since our needs and perspective change over time as we experience new events, we are always in the process of learning to be Christians. We're never finished until we die. So we're always in need of further instruction and nurture. Instruction in Christian faith and practices comes in both programmed and unprogrammed forms.

A church may offer instruction in programmed ways such as worship services, Sunday school classes, confirmation classes, organized Bible study, adult inquiry classes, and special interest small groups. A church may also provide guidance in everyday practices for nurturing faith through prayer, Bible reading, meditation, music, and art.

Instruction in Christian faith and practices also occurs in unprogrammed ways. As we have noted, Lutherans especially point to Word and Sacrament as means through which faith is awakened and fed, but it's not just in formal church worship or study programs that the gospel of Jesus Christ is communicated. It's likely that Christian faith is most frequently learned through personal involvement with Christians who convey convictions about God and Jesus in their words, daily actions, prayers, Bible stories, hymns, family rituals, and service projects. Individuals who have little or no involvement in organized activities of a church have contact with church members. Christian influences are dispersed through many facets of the society. Individuals alienated from a specific institutional church may be presented with Christian faith through certain family members, friends, neighbors, or coworkers. This contemporary form of the priesthood of all believers is exceedingly important. To pray for those who are alienated from the church and to express in a winsome manner the word in life and speech is a vital ministry that cannot be left merely to the clergy. A church as a community of believers scattered through most of the week also gives instruction in the actions and words of its members. In the family this may be quite explicit, in the workplace and broader community it may be more implicit.

2. Lend support for living Christian faith. It is extremely difficult over time for an individual to sustain any belief and way of life without confirmation and support from others. As one of my students commented recently, if she expressed belief that she saw a beautiful tree out her window and the other people with her persistently said there was no tree there, very likely she would begin to doubt the existence of that tree. Sociologists tell us that what we believe to be true is heavily influenced by those around us. This is the case also for any faith and especially so when it is a matter of living with trust in the merciful grace of God, because both our own willful inclinations and the self-help schemes of our culture pull us in the opposite direction. Within each of us is a strong bent to rely more on ourselves or some other worldly thing than on God; to do so is idolatry, and that is the very heart of sin. The pull of idolatry has existed for people of all times and places.

In addition, human cultures have offered multitudinous specific avenues for trusting ultimately in human resources rather than God, and religions or spiritualities have played their part by serving up a wide array of obvious and not-so-obvious self-help schemes. For instance, belief in reincarnation usually runs counter to trust in God's mercy, for reincarnation is most often based on the idea that in the next life we reap what we sowed in this life. Reincarnation is most commonly linked with the idea that spiritual advancement and eventual escape from the cycle of reincarnation depends on the quality of one's life. There is little space for divine mercy here; strict justice and human striving rule. Christian practices and teachings also readily get turned in the direction of idolatry. The simple act of praying every day can be used as an occasion for one's pride, and the doctrine of justification by faith can be used as an instrument for lording it over others. The possibilities for trusting ultimately in human resources are endless. To live with ultimate trust in the merciful grace of God is not easy. To attempt to do so alone is wrought with severe difficulties.

It is vital for anyone drawn to Christian faith to participate in a community that values the stance of trust in God's merciful grace. Of course, there will be no Christian individual or community that embodies this way of life perfectly. Nonetheless, participation in community worship that upholds this stance and regular contact with persons who seek to live with trust in God provide much needed assistance in living this faith. Even with strong community help, it is a struggle to live with trust in God; without community support for this faith, one is almost certain to rely chiefly on human resources, religious or secular.

Some people receive support for Christian faith from a tightly knit circle of family and close friends who are firm Christians, so nearly all the significant people in their lives uphold the same basic outlook. It may even be that most of their close friends attend the same congregation. However, many people in Western societies inhabit a fragmented social world in which many, perhaps all, of their significant others do not hold a Christian view of life. Where can they find affirmation of the Christian outlook? The most obvious place is a church gathered for worship and other activities. Simple attendance at a congregational worship service lends a certain amount of social support; the sheer act of coming together for Christian worship sends a significant message. Special church events can be particularly effective in this regard. Recently I attended an evening of Christmas music during which 1,500 people stood up to join seven choirs singing a Christmas carol. The mass of voices and instruments joined together communicated a strong sense of solidarity in faith. For youth, a week at a church camp can be pivotal. Women's circles or other small groups where people share their faith amidst the struggles of life reinforce one's feeling of belonging with others in this faith. So various organized activities of a church also can serve this purpose of lending social support for Christian faith.

The priesthood of all believers is vital in this arena of social support as well, especially for those persons who are so alienated from the "organized church" that they will not attend one of its functions. It is important for those who affirm the church to undergird the alienated with their prayers and to be good examples of Christian believers. This may be the primary contact the alienated have with the church. Patiently and nondefensively listening to their expressions of disinterest and even hostility toward the church might be part of the healing process; some people have been deeply hurt by the church. It's helpful to remember that most people who drop out of church continue to pray. In fact, one study found that nearly 20 percent of people who identified themselves as atheist (there is no God) or agnostic (I don't know whether or not there is a God) pray daily.[12] Patience, love, good example, and prayer are all valuable. I don't recommend these merely as successful recruiting techniques, for they may not "work." They are basic elements of Christian ministry or priesthood in daily life; this is a high calling indeed. The task of Christians is to carry out this service; the results are up to God and other people.

3. *Provide help and comfort in times of need.* A terrible storm, flood, or war uproots people. Serious illness, death, or divorce throw a person off balance. Job loss, alcohol or drug addiction, depression, physical or sexual abuse, racial or sexual discrimination prompt people to reach out for assistance. The assistance sought in time of need may be that of a trained professional, but it may also be the help that can be given simply by people who care. The church offers both kinds of help. Many denominations sponsor social agencies that offer professional aid. Some parish pastors are trained counselors. Most of all, the church as a community of believers, both when gathered together and when dispersed as individuals, can help those in need. Some Lutheran congregations employ a Steven ministry program to train laypeople to help others who experience loss. One of the fast-growing ways the church has of extending assistance is small groups in which

persons with a common concern such as single parenting come together. Undergirding all the other kinds of help they give, Christians should also provide the support of intercessory prayer.

Although the spirit of individual independence is strong in Western culture, people also have a need and yearning for a supportive faith community. In fact, many people in our society are looking for support in three areas similar to those we have just identified. A recent study of baby boomers age thirty-three to forty-two found that most of them had a market view of churches; that is, they regard churches as offering a product that they are free to buy or not. Another way of putting it is that they look upon the churches as providing resources that they may or may not find useful in their life journey. This group of baby boomers ran the gamut from fundamentalist churchgoers to those who expressed no interest in religion. The study showed that these baby boomer adults are looking for resources in three areas that correspond roughly with the three ways in which the church nurtures Christian faith. First, an astounding 96 percent of the total group said they wanted religious instruction for their children (even 71 percent of the unchurched who said they were not interested in religion agreed). Second, many talked about their need for personal support and reassurance, and often spoke of their need for spiritual guidance and inspiration. These concerns reflect what we have identified as social support for religious faith. Third, many expressed a desire for ties with people on whom they could rely in times of trouble.[13]

Of course, we should not minimize the differences and difficulties. Most boomers are not beating down church doors or crying out specifically for the gospel. What many mean by religious instruction for their children is really just basic morality. Living with trust in God's grace involves radical change, traditionally called repentance, and that does not come easily to anyone. Nevertheless, the church has points of contact in the concerns voiced in the broader culture.

CHRISTIAN SPIRITUALITY AND ECUMENISM

Another issue related to Christian spirituality and the church is ecumenism. That is, the church does not exist as one visible body but as a number of distinct churches or denominations. There is not even just one worldwide Lutheran church. Lutherans are organized into the Evangelical Lutheran Church of Denmark, Evangelical Lutheran Church of Hanover, The Lutheran Church—Missouri Synod, Evangelical Lutheran Church in America, Malagasy Lutheran Church, and so on. How should these various Lutheran churches relate to each other and to churches in other Christian traditions? This is the question about ecumenism. We shall go on to ask what difference the answer makes for Christian spirituality.

The *ecumenical movement* (*ecumenical* is from a Greek word meaning "inhabited world") among Christians began on the foreign mission fields where some questioned the wisdom of perpetuating divisions that had their origins mostly in European history. A number of conferences brought together mission leaders from various Christian traditions, and in 1948 the World Council of Churches was formed. By the time Roman Catholic bishops met in the historic Second Vatican Council (1962–65), the Roman Catholic Church had also sought closer relations with other Christians. Momentous social changes taking place during and after World War II contributed to the ecumenical movement by promoting more contact between people from different churches. In Germany, the common challenges of Nazism and the devastation of war brought Protestants and Catholics closer together. In North America, Europe, and many developing nations, increased movement of people to cities and different parts of the country brought members of previously separated ethnic and religious groups into close proximity with one another. For example, in 1952 the city of Atlanta had only one Roman Catholic Church; in 1980 it had forty-four.

The history of Lutherans in the United States reflects these changes. At one point late in the nineteenth century there were sixty-six different Lutheran denominations, although there were also efforts to build cooperation among regional synods in several broader Lutheran associations. By 1918 there had been many consolidations along ethnic lines, and by 1988 slightly more than 93 percent of American Lutherans were in two churches—the Evangelical Lutheran Church in America and The Lutheran Church—Missouri Synod. However, these two large Lutheran churches exhibit different approaches toward relations with other Lutheran and non-Lutheran churches. These represent two different ecumenical stances.

1. *Seek full agreement in doctrine as the necessary basis for unity.* According to one formulation of this stance, God has already given unity to Christians through their common faith in Jesus Christ; what is lacking is agreement in doctrine. Differences in ceremonies are permissible. Ecumenical endeavors seek to achieve consensus in doctrine. Full agreement in doctrine is necessary, for all the articles of faith are integrally related to the gospel. This is the ecumenical posture of The Lutheran Church—Missouri Synod and several other conservative Lutheran churches in the world.[14]

2. *Seek greater degrees of Christian unity through agreement in the gospel.* This position emphasizes that Lutheranism began as a reform movement that taught in the Augsburg Confessions, Article VII, "For it is sufficient for the true unity of the Christian church that the Gospel be preached in conformity with a pure understanding of it and that the sacraments be administered in accordance with the divine Word."[15] It underscores that agreement in the gospel is *sufficient* for the true unity of the church; differences on many other matters are permitted.[16] With this stance, the Evangelical Lutheran Church in America and many other Lutheran churches around the world have been active in the Lutheran World Federation and World Council of Churches, and established closer relations with a number of other churches, including the Reformed, Episcopal (Anglican), and Roman Catholic.

These two ecumenical stances have already and will continue to produce distinctly different results. Operating with the first stance, The Lutheran Church—Missouri Synod has abstained from involvement in the Lutheran World Federation and World Council of Churches, but cooperates with other church bodies in certain projects that do not involve joint worship or spiritual ministry. While practices regarding participation in Holy Communion vary somewhat in Missouri congregations, the synod's official position is that communion should occur only with those among whom there is doctrinal agreement. Currently The Lutheran Church—Missouri Synod has doctrinal agreement with several churches abroad but none in North America. In the long run, this posture will sustain a very independent Lutheran church quite isolated from other churches.

The second stance already has brought the Evangelical Lutheran Church in America and other Lutheran churches into active participation in both the Lutheran World Federation and the World Council of Churches. Dialogues with theological representatives of the Roman Catholic Church have found considerable, although not complete, agreement on the key issue of justification. The ELCA has also approved intercommunion and sharing of clergy with several churches in the Reformed tradition and with the Episcopal church. In the long haul, the second stance would likely support a unification of Lutherans with Roman Catholics, some other Protestants, and the Orthodox in some sort of reconceived church organization. The key points in this posture are two: (1) agreement in the gospel is sufficient for church unity, and (2) while it is an independent church by default, Lutheranism is most truly a reform movement within the one church.

How should Lutheran Christians and the Lutheran church witness to God's grace in our ecumenical age? The first stance says they should witness to God's grace by standing firmly for truth as expressed in all articles of the Lutheran confessions and an understanding of Scripture as the inerrant word of God. It is not appropriate to paper over differences in doctrine by agreeing to disagree. Confess the truth and expose error is the proper way. The second stance says individual Lutherans and their church should witness to God's grace in this ecumenical age by focusing their attention on the core of Christianity—the gospel of Jesus Christ—and allowing for diversity in other matters of doctrine and practice. One way of seeing the contrast between the two positions is that they differ on how much disagreement is permissible and still have fellowship.

An important ecumenical task among Lutherans today is to keep the lines of communication open between supporters of these two distinct perspectives. It is tempting to feel that the two outlooks have no common ground, yet it is a hopeful sign that the leaders of The Lutheran Church—Missouri Synod and Evangelical Lutheran Church in America continue to communicate with each other.

The two stances affect not only denominations but also the way Christian individuals and congregations nurture and express their faith. Those following the first orientation seek nurture and fellowship almost exclusively with fellow Lutherans among whom there is wide doctrinal agreement. Those following the second orientation will feel free to pray and worship with other Christians whether Lutheran or not. In short, the circle of fellowship with which an individual or congregation finds support is drawn more tightly or more broadly.

In this chapter, our central topic has been the relationship between Christian spirituality and the church. We have seen that Lutheran spirituality is thoroughly communal. A Lutheran understanding of church is nonauthoritarian and stresses its character as a community of believers. The focus of this community of believers is on the means through which faith in Jesus Christ is created, centrally the word and sacraments. A distinctive Lutheran emphasis in regard to the church, and one of its significant contributions to the wider church, is the teaching of the priesthood of all believers. When this is not just an idea but a reality, then God does indeed work through ordinary Christians as they make a witness in their words and actions and as they support others in prayer.

It is a fact, though, that not everyone has a positive experience with the church. Many people are skeptical about church, and the shortcomings and sins of the church have contributed to that skepticism. With humble awareness of its faults, but also with confidence in the gospel, the Christian community needs to clearly make known the good news of Jesus Christ in words, sacraments, and deeds. Gimmicks and fads won't do it.

We human beings have a deeply communal nature that is grounded ultimately in the communal being of God. On one level, we are intricately linked with and dependent on an integrated system of living things in nature. On another level, we have a longing for deep human connections in family and romantic love. On yet another level, there is a hunger within every person for God, whether one calls it that or not. According to core Christian teaching, this communal nature of the world and humans is grounded in God's own communal being. The Christian doctrine of the Trinity implies that there is community within God's own being. What Christian faith has to offer is the wonderfully inviting message of

God as one who reaches out to include us in the community of God's own life, the community of Christian believers, the community of all humankind, and the community of nature. Christian faith is profoundly communal, and integral to this faith is the community of the church.

For Reflection and Practice

1. *Meditation:* From the time line depicting your own experience with the church, pick out the positive experiences with church that have been most significant for you. Some may be frequent and recurring, such as receiving communion; others may be one-time events. How has God touched you through each of these experiences? Give thanks to God for these blessings.

2. *Meditation:* Conflicts within the household of God are not new. King David experienced many difficulties from within Israel and even his own family. Look over the bottom part of your time line produced earlier that identifies the negative experiences you have had with the church. Then open your Bible to Psalm 57 and read through it once. Read the psalm again more slowly, and when any word or phrase speaks to you, dwell on it and let it make connections with your life (this is the method of *lectio divina* used in chapter 2). The basic intention is to let God minister to you and your hurts from the church through the words of this psalm.

3. *Meditation:* What sources feed my faith? Lutheran teaching says that the primary means of grace are word and sacraments. These may or may not be the chief sources of your faith. Reflect on your life and identify the actual sources that feed your faith. How are these sources related to Word and Sacrament?

4. *For reflection and discussion:* To what extent is my congregation a supportive, nurturing faith community? In what areas does it do well? In what areas might it improve?

5. *For reflection and discussion:* At the level of the local congregation, one of the key questions about ecumenical practice is, Who should be welcome to participate in Holy Communion? Churches that uphold the first ecumenical stance welcome only those people who are members from a church that shares full doctrinal agreement with them. Churches with the second stance receive at communion people from churches that affirm the gospel of Jesus Christ and the

real presence of Christ in the eucharist. However, local practice may vary. What do you think is the appropriate practice for admission to Holy Communion? What are your reasons?

6. *For reflection and discussion:* Give your own assessment of the two major ecumenical stances among Lutherans; identify specific strengths and weaknesses. What do you think is the proper ecumenical stance for a Lutheran denomination today? What are your reasons?

7

CHURCH TRADITIONS

C HURCHES HAVE MANY TRADITIONS. It's true both of local congregations and of whole denominations. It's true also of Lutheran churches. Attitudes toward church traditions vary greatly. Some folks cling tightly to even the smallest of local traditions such as a certain manner of ringing the church bell before services; to them familiar ways are the best. Some others are very impatient with church traditions, for they feel the old patterns smother creativity. Both groups see church tradition like a well-traveled road, although they experience that road differently. Those who hold fast to the traditions believe that traditions are the surest route to reach their goal. Those who are suspicious of church traditions feel that traditions prevent exploration of new, interesting territory. What roles should church traditions play in our contemporary cultural situation? This is what we want to consider.

For three reasons that we have touched on before, we may feel considerable uncertainty about what route to take in spiritual matters. One reason is that our highly pluralistic religious context makes it hard to know which direction to go. Think of all the religious/spiritual options available in a large city. There are well-known as well as obscure Christian churches. There are places for astrological and tarot readings, along with organized New Age groups. Almost every major religion in the world is represented. Then there are possible substitutes for an explicitly religious or spiritual group such as social change movements intended to overcome poverty, racism, sexism, abuse of nature, and so forth. Plus militant antireligious societies. A bewildering number of choices confronts us. In which of these options will we participate?

A second reason it is difficult to find our way in spiritual matters today lies within rather than outside us, and that is our very strong emphasis upon personal choice. Most of us in Western culture today feel that the self is rather malleable, like Play-doh that can be shaped and reshaped. In fact, we tend to believe that one of our major tasks on the journey of life is to mold ourselves. Hence, the choices we make about spiritual/religious groups are also choices about what sort of person we will become. With this sense of responsibility for shaping our own identity, we are less inclined to follow the path of our elders simply out of inertia or habit. We are more open to exploring various options.

The result for many people is the third reason for greater difficulty in finding our way—more elective ties with religious institutions. This is a new state of affairs, this combination of a social environment filled with diverse options, an internal sense of self that stresses personal choice and exploration of options, and more elective ties with religious institutions.

We can get a sense of how the situation has changed if we compare the experience of Grandmother Paulene and her granddaughter Rachel. Paulene was born in 1903 on a farm in west central Minnesota, where she grew up; she married and raised a family on a farm about three miles from where she was born. Her entire family—parents and siblings—and her husband's entire family lived within a radius of fifteen miles. All but one person of this extended family were Lutheran, although they belonged to different congregations. One of her sisters brought about a major crisis when she married a Roman Catholic and joined his church. Although the family finally accepted it, there was still some awkwardness when they attended baptisms, confirmations, weddings, or funerals at the other church. Paulene used to be suspicious of Roman Catholics and Pentecostals (in her youth she sometimes called them "mackerel snappers" and "holy rollers"), although she thought of Methodists, Presbyterians, and Baptists as just doing things a bit differently. There was never a question in her mind that she would be anything other than Lutheran, and she assumed that her children would be Lutheran. For the most part, Paulene lived within a Lutheran world, certainly within a Christian world. To be sure, there were some people within the community who did not belong to any church, but none of them publicly promoted a different view of things. Until she was over fifty years old, she commonly encountered prayers and hymns at local civic and school gatherings, and the radio and films represented similar occurrences elsewhere in the country.

Granddaughter Rachel was born in 1973 and grew up mostly in a suburb of St. Paul, Minnesota, where she quite regularly attended a Lutheran church until age six, at which point her parents divorced. When her mother remarried several years later, Rachel became part of a blended family. Her stepfather had loose ties with the Methodist church. The family seldom went to church; the parents decided just to let the children choose whether they wanted to join a church when they got older. When she was in junior high school, Rachel was confirmed at a Lutheran church largely because one of her friends went there. After confirmation, Rachel dropped out of church. This continued during college when she followed the custom of most other students of sleeping in on Sunday mornings. Among her college acquaintances she counted Jews, Muslims, Hindus, and Buddhists. She also knew some students who frequented a bookstore that specialized in New Age materials. She encountered some faculty and students who criticized Christianity as incompatible with modern science, and met others who saw it as authoritarian and repressive.

After graduating from college, Rachel moved to Denver, Colorado, in order to be close to good ski slopes. There she now works with a nonobservant Jew, a devout Presbyterian, a lapsed Mormon, and a man who talks in puzzling ways about crystals. Everyday she drives by a mosque. In college and afterward in Denver she has had romantic ties with men who varied widely in religious outlook—from indifferent to Evangelical Christian. On top of these personal contacts, contemporary media has influenced Rachel all her life. As a child, she watched a Saturday morning television cartoon called *Isis* whose central character by that name is well known in occult groups as an ancient Egyptian figure with magical powers into which today's initiated can tap. As an adult, Rachel reads in her newspaper a comic strip that presents a running story about a character who undergoes frequent reincarnation. Rachel lives in a pluralistic world, a world where people with many different religions and views of life interact.

What is it like to *experience* a pluralistic world in which one feels one has many choices? We can get some sense of that by comparing Grandmother Paulene's experience of her Christian world with Rachel's life in a pluralistic world. For Grandmother Paulene, the Lutheran Church was a *given*. She approached life and its many decisions with the assumption of a Christian outlook as that embodied in the Lutheran community of her time and place. Not that people talked constantly about God from this Lutheran perspective; most of the time it was simply taken for granted as the unspoken framework of life. This meant, though, that Paulene entered every situation with the conviction that the Lutheran-Christian outlook represented the norm of truth and goodness. It was possible for someone to dissent or depart from that tradition, as her sister had done when she became Catholic, but that was unusual. Even then her sister stayed within Christianity. In any case, Paulene began with the assumption that Christianity and the Lutheran tradition are the standard of truth.

On the other hand, Christianity and the Lutheran church do not have the same sort of *given* quality for Rachel. They are a starting point for her, since that was what she knew as a young girl until age six and then during confirmation instruction. But neither her parents nor she have the same presumption as existed in Grandmother Paulene's day, that the children will, of course, continue in this faith tradition. Rachel feels she has many religious/spiritual options to choose from; she is free to steer her life however she wishes. Here we see exemplified the three factors we have identified as greater religious pluralism, increased personal autonomy, and more elective ties with religious institutions.

These social forces have a powerful impact upon people's sense of what is true or *plausible*. When something is called plausible, it is considered believable, likely, and feasible, and hence one tends to accept it as true. Something branded implausible is regarded as unbelievable, unlikely, and incredible, so one tends to reject it as false. Sociologists point out that what we think is plausible is heavily dependent upon the support of other people who share the same belief. This is true of all our beliefs, not just religious beliefs. For instance, people with some education in modern science believe that the earth and other planets in the solar system revolve around the sun. We believe this even though very few of us have ever verified that belief with firsthand experience. You and I believe it because we live within a society that honors the views of modern science. People of other times and cultures have held different beliefs about the planets and sun. Of course, we are prone to assume that we have the complete truth about the solar system, but the odds are very good that future generations will hold modified beliefs about it. This does not trouble us, for probably we will not be alive to rub shoulders with people affirming a divergent belief about the solar system.

It's a far different situation, though, when it comes to beliefs about the whole scheme in which human life takes place. Such beliefs are basic to religion, spirituality, or a philosophy of life. Here is where dramatic and fundamental change has taken place from Grandmother Paulene's world to Rachel's world. Grandmother Paulene had virtually no contact with people who held a conflicting worldview. While she knew there were people in the world with contrasting religious beliefs, they did not enter into her experience. The situation for Rachel is profoundly altered. She experiences the world as filled with a tremendous variety of views about the nature of reality and the purpose of human life. Whereas Grandmother Paulene experienced the Christian worldview as the highly plausible outlook that she was strongly disposed to hold as true, Granddaughter Rachel experiences Christianity as one among a number of possible perspectives on life.

In the world of Grandmother Paulene, church traditions were respected and followed, sometimes without reflecting on them. Frequently this included local traditions such as holding the church ice cream social on the last Sunday in June. But what place do church traditions have in Rachel's world, which is filled with traditions from many different religions and secular belief systems? This is our question. What is the role of church traditions today? We will look first at what the Lutheran tradition itself says about church traditions.

CORE CHURCH TRADITIONS

The Lutheran confessional writings make an imprecise yet useful distinction between core church traditions that are vital to Christian faith and secondary traditions that may be useful but are not essential. The difference is like that between the trunk of a tree and its branches. The tree can lose some branches and still survive; in fact, it will grow new branches. If the trunk is seriously harmed, however, the entire tree will die. Core church traditions constitute the trunk of Christian faith. The arrangement of topics in the Augsburg Confession, the earliest and most widely acknowledged Lutheran statement, reflect this distinction. In the first three articles of the Augsburg Confession, Lutherans affirm commonly recognized Christian teachings about the Trinity, sin, and the person of Jesus Christ. Article IV treats justification, and statements about the church, baptism, the Lord's supper, and confession/absolution follow. These belong to the core. Among secondary traditions are church ceremonies and practices instituted by human authority.

The first of the core traditions named in the Augsburg Confession is the doctrine of the Trinity, which has strong roots in the New Testament and was formally approved at two ecumenical church councils in the fourth century. This is a tradition that Lutherans and most other Christians say belongs to the trunk of Christian faith. While the doctrine of the Trinity may sound like some trick with numbers, the teaching really says that in addition to being the source of all, God is fully and truly present in Jesus Christ and the Holy Spirit. So to have faith in Jesus Christ is to have an intimate relationship with the merciful God. This issue—whether Jesus is central for personally knowing the depths of God's love and mercy—is very alive today.

In our pluralistic world the significance of Jesus is seriously debated. There is a range of views, but three basic answers are given to this question. One widely held view is that *Jesus is one of many equally true ways of relating to God.* Many who endorse this view would agree with this baby boomer's opinion, "I don't think it matters what religion you are in as long as you are comfortable with it and following sound principles, you are raising your kids and spending time with your family, and you are moral. Then it doesn't matter."[1] This is a form of relativism, for what is considered true is entirely relative to the culture or the individual and, most importantly, one religious view is as true as another. It is also a form of theological pluralism, for it holds that there is a plurality of equally true views of God.[2] This approach can be expressed as *relativistic pluralism.*

Inevitably, relativistic pluralism has implications for one's view of Jesus. Jesus is one of a number of equally good religious leaders. However, the baby boomer just quoted recognizes two criteria for evaluating religion. One criterion is that "you are comfortable with it." This emphasizes not only that religion is a personal choice but that religion should be satisfying and trouble free. The second criterion introduces a moral standard by which all religions may be evaluated, namely, that you are "following sound principles, you are raising your kids and spending time with your family, and you are moral." Thus this person is relativistic about the truth of religions, but claims there is a universal moral standard.[3] In fact, relativistic pluralism regards morality as the essential contents of religion; everything else is external packaging that varies with culture and is dispensable. Many would express this moral content, in loftier terms, as love.

Another way of expressing relativistic pluralism in religion or spirituality is that one will say, "Christianity is true *for me,* but Buddhism is true *for Buddhists.*" Proponents of this perspective often cite a story about two ants on an elephant that goes like this. On an ear of the elephant, one ant says, "An elephant is like an ear—thin, vulnerable, and sensitive to even soft sounds." Another ant on one of the elephant's feet says, "No, an elephant is like a large hoof—thick, strong, and tough." The point of the story is that what both ants say is true; furthermore, it is said that one is not more true than the other. Just as little ants see only a very small portion of the big elephant, so we humans experience just a little part of the immense God.

A sociological study of baby boomers found that those who hold to relativistic pluralism feel faith is a very private concern. They generally avoid trying to pass on their faith to other people, even their children. In their households religious faith is seldom discussed, and there is little observance of religious practices such as common prayer at mealtime and bedtime. Inescapably though, the parental emphasis on private, personal choice in a relativistic world is the prevailing atmosphere in which their children grow up.[4]

A second answer to the question about Jesus is that *Jesus is the one true way to relate to God.* Other religions and their leaders are regarded as basically misguided. It is admitted that other religions may have moral strengths and a very limited grasp of truth about God, but faith in Jesus is necessary for salvation. A key Scripture passage for this viewpoint is John 14:6, "Jesus said to him, 'I am the way, and the truth, and the life. No one comes to the Father except through me.'" Another important verse is Acts 4:12, "There is salvation in no one else, for there is no other name under heaven given among mortals by which we must be saved." This point of view is often called *Christian exclusivism,* for it holds that Jesus is the only path to salvation. Those with a Christian exclusivist perspective usually are intent upon winning others to Christian faith and very concerned to pass on their religious beliefs and practices to their children. Since exclusivists believe it matters greatly what religious faith one has, they earnestly seek to have others affirm the truth of Jesus.

A third view of the significance of Jesus is that *Jesus is the fullest truth.* This outlook has a more positive estimate of other religions and faiths, for it holds that many elements of truth about God may be present outside of Christian faith. Yet it believes that Jesus is the fullest revelation of God and hence is most true. This view is often called *Christian inclusivism.*[5] This differs from relativism in that Christian inclusivism claims openly that there are different degrees of truth in religion and spirituality and that Jesus is the fullest truth. Inclusivism differs from exclusivism in having a more appreciative opinion of other religions/spiritualities and also in remaining open to the possibility of ultimate salvation for those without faith in Jesus. On this last point, Christian inclusivists point out that in addition to the message of John 14:6 and Acts 4:12 that stress Jesus as the one way of salvation, there is another set of passages that say final judgment is based on a person's deeds (Matthew 25:31-46; Romans 2:6-8; 2 Corinthians 5:10; 1 Peter 1:17) and a third set of passages that suggest that through the abundant mercy of God revealed in Christ all people will eventually be saved (Romans 5:18; 11:32).

This diversity of views about Jesus reflects our complex world of social pluralism. It's difficult to know how to respond to such diversity among Christians as well as the multiplicity of faiths in the world. To be sure, almost everyone wants to avoid compulsion in matters of faith and especially persecution and fighting between groups with different religious convictions. This is where relativistic pluralism seems so appealing, for it appears to satisfy everyone. In effect, it says, "Take whatever religious/spiritual belief and practice you like; it doesn't matter as long as you are a moral person." On the other hand, many are concerned to be faithful to their religious/spiritual faith and tradition. They wonder, Is it really true that spirituality or religion simply boils down to morality?

Here is where attention to the church's tradition of trinitarian doctrine will prompt one to pause and examine the consequences of taking the route of relativistic pluralism in which Jesus is one of many equally good ways of relating to God. While Jesus is regarded as a great religious/moral teacher, so are many others. One far-reaching consequence of this view is that God ends up seeming very distant and nebulous. If Jesus, the Buddha, Lao-tzu, Madame Blavatsky, and many others are equally reliable guides to God's character, then only what they hold in common is most solid. What these highly diverse teachers hold in common, however, is very little. For instance, scholars generally believe that the Buddha never spoke of "God." So if one is going to speak about Ultimate Reality at all (and some Buddhists do not), one can do so only in very abstract terms. To be sure, some people are drawn to such abstractness. I recently encountered a physician who spoke with enthusiasm about "the Essence" behind every religion and spirituality. However, one cannot say anything particular about "the Essence." The Essence must be very mysterious and transcendent.

Now, it is indeed true that God is mysterious and transcends all our words and images. However, Jesus leads us to believe that God is not only transcendent and mysterious, but also loving and merciful. If this view about the Essence is *as true* as what Jesus shows us, then the message about God's love and mercy is just extra baggage that should be discarded. If God is above all transcendent and mysterious, then our relationship with God can only be rather distant. We may have awe and respect for such a deity, but there won't be much trust and gratitude. But when Jesus is taken as *the decisive* revelation of God, then God is understood as loving to the extent of sharing directly in our suffering and as merciful by accepting us and opening up new possibilities of life. When Jesus is central, then it's possible to have a close relationship with the loving, merciful God. So it's not just our *ideas about* God that are at stake, but the very nature of our *relationship* with God.

Another closely related consequence of going the road of relativistic pluralism is that the good news of the gospel is replaced with a message that places the primary burden of liberation/salvation on our own shoulders. To be sure, shouldering this burden is a popular move, for it fits perfectly with some of the key elements of our alienated condition. As we saw in chapter 2, a basic ingredient in our alienation is that we trust more in human resources than in God. Religion or spirituality is not free from this tendency. In fact, religion or spirituality themselves readily become tools of this human effort to avoid giving our lives to God by putting the weight of liberation/salvation on ourselves. Jesus the Lord and Savior is replaced by a Jesus who is one of many teachers whose good example and instruction we may strive to follow.

The doctrine of the Trinity is a church tradition that continues to play a vital role as an indicator of a critical choice in possible routes for our spiritual journey. trinitarian doctrine should not be used as a club to force people to follow a certain line, for we need to make up our own minds freely. It helps to remember that Christians are not asked to put their faith in the *doctrine* of the Trinity. Faith should be in God, not a doctrine. The core tradition of trinitarian doctrine can serve the useful function, though, of asking what sort of God we put our faith in. Do we believe in a distant God who lays the burden of salvation on us? The doctrine of the Trinity says when Jesus is taken as the key to God, then we put our faith in the God of merciful love who opens up fresh possibilities beyond our own moral resources.[6]

Secondary Church Traditions

In addition to core church traditions, there are many secondary traditions, which may be useful but are not essential. At the time of the Reformation, questions were raised especially about many devotional and worship practices common in the Roman Catholicism of that era. For instance, Roman Catholics were expected to fast during Lent, and their communal worship followed a liturgical form usually called the Western or Roman rite, in distinction from rites of the Eastern

Orthodox church. The question arose among Lutherans whether they should observe the traditional Catholic worship and devotional practices. What the Lutherans did with worship rites exemplifies their approach.

Lutherans continued to use the Western rite liturgy with some modifications mostly in practices associated with it. Whereas the liturgy had been entirely in Latin, Lutherans began to use the people's own language where Latin was not understood. Congregational singing was reinstituted. Instead of the medieval practice of giving only bread to the laity in Holy Communion, they were now given wine also.[7] Lutherans also removed eucharistic prayers that suggested that the eucharist was offered to God as a sacrifice for sin in the sense of a good work done by humans. The end result was that the basic structure of the Western rite liturgy was retained.

The basic policy was to retain traditional practices that were consistent with a relationship with God based on God's merciful grace, for there was no good reason to unnecessarily disturb people during the Reformation era with its massive upheavals in the church. As Philip Melanchthon put it, "Nothing should be changed in the accustomed rites without good reason, and to foster harmony those ancient customs should be kept that can be kept without sin or without great disadvantage."[8] The critical question raised about any secondary religious tradition was whether it conflicted with a core tradition. During the Reformation period, core teachings about the Trinity and Jesus Christ were not disputed by the major parties, so Lutherans focused their attention on whether a practice was consistent with the core doctrine of justification. They retained the Western rite liturgy or mass except for portions of the eucharistic prayer that they believed incompatible with a sound understanding of justification. This is why there is such striking similarity yet today between a traditional Lutheran eucharistic service and the Roman Catholic mass.[9] Of course, the music will most often differ, but the underlying structure of the liturgy is the same.

Forms of corporate worship have become a topic of spirited discussion today as well. Naturally, ours is a different situation than the early sixteenth century. Many, such as pastor and church administrator David Luecke, argue that fresh worship patterns are needed to connect the Christian message with people who are untouched, even bored, by traditional Lutheran liturgical forms. Those who take this position often stress what they call alternative or contemporary worship. These services vary, but some features frequently appear. Informality is prized; for example, the pastor may use a folksy style of speech and may dress casually rather than in vestments or clerical collar. Another feature is some sort of "contemporary music." Although there is music written today for symphony orchestras or organ (and so contemporary), what is usually meant is some other musical form such as soft rock, pop, folk, or jazz. The words of the songs are generally simple and easy to learn. Sometimes the informality of the setting encourages people to sway and clap their hands along with the music. Frequently, less Scripture is read than the three lessons customarily used in the traditional liturgy today, although a fairly long sermon is common. The pastor often does not preach from a pulpit. If there is a eucharist, there is frequently no substantial eucharistic prayer; just the words of institution ("On the night in which he was betrayed Jesus took bread . . ."). Advocates of such contemporary worship say it more readily connects with peoples' lives today.[10]

Others counter that the historic Western rite liturgy is the best way to instill sound Christian faith. For instance, pastor and liturgical scholar Frank Senn argues that alternative worship services have roots in rationalism and revivalism. The rationalist influence is evident in the lack of rich symbolism in either language or ritual; everything in the service is intended to be straightforward and immediately understandable by everyone. Another sign of rationalism is to organize the worship service around popular themes in the culture (Mother's Day or ecology) rather than around the biblical texts of the church year. Senn says the influence of revivalism is seen in a stress on enthusiasm and conversion experiences, but little attention to sound Christian doctrine. While conversions of great Christian leaders such as Augustine and Luther led to fresh formulations of Christian doctrine, those converted through revivalism just look for more stimulating religious experiences. Furthermore, Senn says many alternative services with praise music reflect revivalism's concentration on Jesus almost to the exclusion of the Father and Holy

Spirit. Senn's overriding point is that a worship service always conveys a message. The question is, What message should Christian worship bring? Senn argues that most alternative worship services have a meaning that simply reinforces assumptions present in the culture. Christian worship should rather express the gospel of Jesus Christ and be firmly trinitarian; the best available forms for that are the historic liturgy and hymns.[11]

There is a wide range of opinion regarding corporate worship today, wider than a few paragraphs can express. At one extreme are those who support services with so little Christian content that the main emphasis is on morality and being a better person. At the other extreme are those who think it is enough to follow mechanically the same order of service year after year. Obviously, neither David Luecke nor Frank Senn advocate these extremes. Luecke believes it is possible to have alternative worship services that convey the good news of Jesus Christ, and Senn stresses that a traditional Western rite liturgy can be done with vitality and a sense of the wonder of God.

In addition to the basic order of worship, there are ethnic and cultural factors that influence worship. For instance, African Americans are likely to do the Western rite liturgy of the *Lutheran Book of Worship* in a different way than German Americans using the same book. When still other musical and verbal settings of the Western rite enter the picture, there are more possibilities than might at first be evident. Similar things could be said about a specific alternative worship order. Liturgical scholar James White calls these matters of *style*, and says a worship tradition can be quite elastic in accommodating varying styles.[12]

So what should we do about worship today? This is not a choice between tradition and some complete innovation. Rather, this is a choice among different traditions within the church. On the one hand, use of the Western rite liturgy goes back to the early centuries of Christianity and was reaffirmed at the Reformation as a secondary tradition. On the other hand, Frank Senn is correct in tracing the basic elements of most alternative worship services not only to the traditions of revivalism and rationalism in Western culture generally but also to the pietist tradition within Lutheranism itself. Lutheran pietism encouraged less formal, heartfelt worship as well as warm hymns and songs that people loved to sing at a prayer meeting or around a campfire. All these—Western rite and alternative—are secondary church traditions.

The Lutheran reformer Philip Melanchthon referred to secondary religious traditions by the Latin word *adiaphora,* which means "nonessential." The term *adiaphora* (pronounced ah-dee-ah-for-ah) has the advantage of stressing that Christians have freedom in regard to secondary religious traditions; that is, Christians may or may not follow them without necessarily compromising faith in Jesus Christ. Hence, Christians are free to use an Eastern Orthodox liturgy, the Western rite liturgy, or some alternative rite. The disadvantage of the term *adiaphora* is that it might suggest that what a community or individual does in regard to worship "makes no difference." That would be wrong. It makes a huge difference what forms of worship are employed, for those forms inevitably communicate something. We need to ask several serious questions about worship services we attend or plan.

First, *what message* is being sent? The key issue is whether the worship pattern chosen is compatible with core Christian traditions. So one needs to ask, Does the good news of God's merciful grace in Jesus Christ come through strongly? If Jesus shares relatively equal time with other religious leaders or if the dominant message is about what we can do to be good people, then it's something other than Christian worship.

Second, does the service *communicate* the intended message, does it succeed in reaching people? On the deepest level, this is a matter led by the Holy Spirit, for we cannot control whether the gospel message touches someone's heart. Nevertheless, there are some outward signs that give us clues. Congregants watching the performance of an alternative service passively or completing a Western rite liturgy listlessly, and routinely are indicators that the Christian message is not getting through. It's not just what forms are used, but *how* they are used. People who attend a worship service over an extended time tend to be shaped by what happens there for them. Persons who are touched by the message of God's merciful grace participate more and more fully in that relationship with God. But those who experience only emptiness or boredom have negative attitudes toward Christian faith formed in them, and those who have pleasant experiences without encountering the gospel have mistaken notions about Christian faith reinforced.

Third, *with whom* does a worship service communicate or fail to communicate? It may be that certain groups of people are reached by one kind of service and not by another, yet one cannot know this without some experimentation and observation. For instance, in one church that offers a Western rite liturgy and alternative service at different times on Sunday morning for one year and then next year reverses the times, the pastor has found that the foremost factor in people's choice was time, not the kind of service.

In this chapter, we have seen that church traditions are not all on the same level of significance. The Lutheran tradition includes a cluster of traditions, and it distinguishes between core traditions and secondary traditions. A core tradition such as the doctrine of the Trinity is shared with nearly all other Christian churches. We have seen that one prime concern of this doctrine is to emphasize the centrality of Jesus for understanding God and ourselves. In today's world, with its multitude of religious and spiritual traditions readily available, the centrality of Jesus Christ is a beacon that shows the surest route for Christians to follow and alerts them to diversions.

When true to itself, Lutheranism offers freedom, as well as respect toward secondary church traditions. Lutherans are free to draw upon practices in their own tradition, in other churches, or even in other religious traditions, as long as those practices are consistent with the core traditions. This is true of worship as well as practices of prayer and devotion. Worship expert James White says that the ability to borrow from other traditions may be a sign of strength and self-confidence rather than weakness or confusion.[13] I have suggested that Lutheran churches are free to use either the Western rite or alternative services. The critical test is that the worship service be thoroughly grounded in the message of God's grace in Jesus Christ.

For Reflection and Practice

1. Draw a picture that expresses your current relationship with God and with Jesus. After you have finished the drawing, examine it. What does the picture tell you about the nature of these relationships?

2. Draw a picture that expresses how you believe God relates to Christians and followers of other religions.

After you have finished the drawing, does it reflect an understanding like relativistic pluralism, exclusivism, or inclusivism? What are your reasons for holding this view? Can you identify any Scripture passages that support your view?

3. Authentic Christian worship is not an attempt to catch God's attention, but is first of all a response of thanks and praise for who God is and what God has done. Are there any things outside worship services that elicit from you a response to God of thanks and praise? What elements of the worship services in which you have participated evoke your thanks and praise to God?

4. In your estimation, how important are the following factors for Christian corporate worship: (a) preparation by worship leaders, (b) preparation of each worshiper (e.g., quieting down, prayer), (c) the type of worship service used (e.g., Western rite, alternative service, etc.), (d) the music, (e) other.

5. For the past six months, Julie has not been getting anything out of the worship services at her church. What do you think she should do: stop going to church, look around for another church, complain to the pastor, make an appointment with the pastor or respected Christian to talk, or something else?

If the above exercises and questions are completed with a group, they will involve people more fully when individuals have time alone first. Individuals may then share their drawings or reflections with others in small groups before coming together as a total group.

8

SERVICE IN DAILY LIFE

L
UTHERAN SPIRITUALITY INVOLVES NOT ONLY a number of
religious practices, but it is also a faith that informs the stuff of everyday life. We've understood spirituality as a faith plus a path. That is, a spirituality is a living faith that is nurtured and expressed by certain practices
that together make up a spiritual path. We've also seen that a spirituality
with faith in God will have a theology, a certain way of understanding
God and our relationship with God. It's clear that Lutheran spirituality is
closely linked with major points in Lutheran theology. So after considering the depth of our human predicament, we focused on the heart of
Lutheran spirituality—a faith relationship with God centered on trust in
God's merciful grace made known in Jesus. Next we looked at the chief
religious realities that nurture this faith relationship: various forms of the
word of God, sacraments, and the fellowship of Christians. These practices—attention to the word in Scripture, sermons, witness of ordinary
Christians, key doctrines, as well as to baptism and eucharist—are the
core traditions of Lutheran spirituality. There are also many secondary
traditions that may express and nourish this faith relationship, but these
traditions in music, worship, prayer, or group organization may vary considerably from culture to culture. The heart of the matter is the faith relationship with God.

Now we come to another major element of Lutheran spirituality—how the faith relationship with God finds expression in daily life.
In brief, the biblical answer is that faith is active in love. Or to put it
another way, faith in Jesus Christ manifests itself through service to
others. How this happens is the subject of this chapter. We start with
a theological vision of how God is related to the stuff of everyday life.
The vision has three strands of thought.

146

God's Presence in Daily Life

God possesses worldly rule. God as creator not only gives existence to the world and all living things, but also provides the conditions for life to continue. We tend to think of God the creator being active at the beginning of the world and maybe at the start of our individual lives, but that is a very limited view. God's creative activity is ongoing, for God also sustains the world in each moment of time. This work of continuous creation merges with what we call God's providence, namely, God's ongoing care for creatures. A significant part (but only part) of God's ongoing creativity is to provide order for the world.[1] The sciences study especially the order present in nature. We call various elements of that order "laws of nature." The law of gravity is perhaps most familiar to us, but there are many laws of nature. What is the source of this rational, lawlike character of the universe? Atheists say there is no explanation; it has just happened. Those who believe in God say the source is the mind and will of God.

God's creative activity of providing order extends also into human life. The Ten Commandments give lawlike expression to some of this intended order. Although we may think of the Ten Commandments as rules arbitrarily imposed by a divine ruler, they have much more in common with the laws of nature. That is, a law of nature such as the law of gravity expresses a regularity or order *built into* the universe by God. The order is there first; what we formulate as a law of nature is an effort to describe that order. Similarly, the commandments not to kill, steal, commit adultery, or lie are not arbitrarily imposed on human beings who might live just as well by following contrary patterns. No, given the fact that human beings are created as social beings who need one another, human life is better when people avoid killing, stealing, adultery, and lying. Just as there is an order built into atoms by God, so there is an order or structure to human beings. Moral laws such as the second part of the Ten Commandments and moral teachings of other religions give expression to that order. This structure is also apparent to human reason, so moral philosophy and legal thought may also articulate it.

These fundamental moral teachings identify some essential conditions for humans to live well while carrying out basic functions. One such function is to bear and raise the young; since this is a cooperative enterprise, some sort of family is necessary. To obtain food, clothing, and shelter, we also need to work, and generally we divide up different tasks. Partly for protection we also gather into larger social units and devise some way to organize that society. These basic activities of family, work, and common life are grounded in our nature and are shared by all humans. However, the particular forms of family, work, and common life may vary greatly with time and place. An ancient Roman family with its autocratic father bears little resemblance to a contemporary Italian two-career family. First-century China had no computer programmers or automobile mechanics, and there is little call for chariot makers in contemporary China. In Africa adult Ndebele men and women under King Mzilikazi during the first half of the nineteenth century had different roles in public life than today's Ndebele citizens in Zimbabwe. While the specific forms of family, work, and common life vary, these functions are basic to human life together.

Martin Luther said that the performance of these basic functions of human life is part of God's continuing care for the creation. That is, God works in and through persons and their social roles to provide the care necessary for human life to continue. Luther said everyone has certain "stations" or "offices"; we would call them social roles. For instance, a woman may have certain stations in her family (daughter, sister, wife, mother), other stations in the realm of paid work (real estate salesperson, supervisor, coworker), and still other stations in the wider community (voter, chair of a neighborhood committee). Luther's point is that God's intent for each constructive social role is that a person serve the needs of others in and through that role. God does not directly feed babies, supply telephone service, or put out house fires, but God does these things indirectly through the actions of people carrying out their roles in society. Luther refers to the parent, telephone service person, and firefighter as "masks of God." Through these human masks God provides for the needs of people.

Each station or social role has responsibilities associated with it, a set of "oughts" and "ought nots," of "musts" and "must nots." For instance, my work as a college teacher involves leadership of classes, grading exams and papers, and advising students. If I did not perform these tasks in a satisfactory manner, the academic dean would call me to account. I could lose my position. In a more positive light, these "oughts" and "ought nots" express the basic ways I can serve students. The basic responsibilities of my position as teacher are spelled out in the *Luther College Faculty Handbook*, which is a legal document. Beyond that, my own conscience holds me to a higher standard of what it means to be a college teacher. But behind both the rules of the faculty handbook and the internalized law of my conscience lies the will and law of God that declares that I am to serve the good of my students. So Luther says God carries on this work of continuing creation through law. God's law is the ultimate standard, and the laws of governments, rules of other institutions, societal morality, and the dictates of our consciences are at best approximations of divine law and at worst contradictions of it.

The main point here is that God does not need somehow to be inserted by us into the various routines and relationships of our daily life, for God is already present and active there as continuous creator. God has made us social beings who need one another in a host of ways, and God's will that we serve one another is manifested in various degrees in the duties of our social roles. Indeed, every constructive social role is a mask behind which the Creator, hidden, meets the needs of people. All this is true whether or not one believes in God, and often even whether or not one intends to serve others. The cook in a fast-food restaurant helps meet a need of others even though the cook does it merely for the pay. For the most part, it's different in family life, because such intimate relationships cannot effectively endure without some genuine concern for the other. But in work and public life it is possible for someone acting entirely out of selfish motives to benefit others simply through the skillful performance of duty. This divine activity of continuous creation belongs to what Luther calls "God's worldly kingdom or rule." This is God's way of governing all human life, for here all who carry out the responsibilities of their constructive social roles are instruments of God, whether they know it or not.

Evil distorts. Our picture of the Creator's presence and activity in daily life would not be complete without acknowledging that God contends with the power of evil in the world. God's governance is constantly challenged by contrary forces. For instance, people kill one another or fail to carry out the duties of their social roles, or less grievously, they fulfill their social roles partly or totally out of selfishness. A major difference between laws of nature and laws of society is that there is no possibility for us to defy a natural law without immediate negative effects. If we try to ignore the law of gravity by walking off the top of a building, we will immediately pay a heavy price. It is possible, though, for a person to steal without noticing bad results; indeed, the immediate outcome for the thief may appear very good. Behavior that breaks state and moral law is so common and persistent that human societies have always devised various control and enforcement mechanisms in an attempt to contain the destructive effects. Police, courts, and prisons are among our contemporary mechanisms, although no social control apparatus eliminates the problem. According to Luther, persons who perform the proper functions of the police, courts, and prisons are also masks of God through which God opposes evil. This is part of what Luther calls the "strange work" of God.

Evil infects not only persons but also social institutions and social roles themselves. The power of the police is used sometimes to subvert justice. The structure of family life has commonly been twisted to the advantage of males. Traditional social roles for women have restricted them. Slavery has been institutionalized in many societies and exists even today. Some social roles such as drug dealer and pimp are thoroughly evil. At best, the social roles we fill are ambiguous; that is, while they generally have the potential for doing good, they are also flawed. Social roles, even when constructive, are a mixture of good and evil.[2]

Evil is not limited to persons, social roles, and institutions, for in Luther's view, behind them is Satan. The kingdom or rule of Satan is opposed to God's rule. People are caught in the middle between these two greater powers, and we serve either one or the other. Martin Luther had a vivid sense of the reality and power of Satan, as did the apostle Paul. Most people in Western cultures today do not have such a lively sense of a personal leader of evil, and it may not be necessary to believe in the existence of a personal devil. What Satan represents, though, is a power of evil vastly greater than we humans can control, and such a conviction about the seriousness of evil is part and parcel of Lutheran spirituality. This conviction is the deeply felt belief that we humans are unable to free ourselves from the power of evil. Only God is able to free us. One of the ways God opposes evil is through God's worldly rule, which makes use of social roles and laws to serve the good of creatures.

Why do people hurt one another and break moral laws? Why do distorted social roles develop and persist? Many answers are offered. Some say it's bad parenting, poverty, or the media. Others point to selfishness or greed. There is some truth in these and other suggestions. As we have seen in chapter 2, Christian faith goes much deeper and says the root of the problem is that we human beings are alienated from God. As Augustine said long ago in a prayer, "Thou hast made us for Thyself, and we are restless until we find our rest in thee." "Thou hast made us for Thyself" suggests that human beings are intended for relationship with God. This is an order or structure built into us. The First Commandment gives expression to this order in terms of a negative law, "You shall have no other gods before me." Jesus put it in positive terms, "You shall love the Lord your God with all your heart and soul and mind." One of the interesting results in recent scientific research into the relation between health and spirituality is solid evidence that, on average, religious people are healthier than the nonreligious. Harvard Medical School Professor Herbert Benson even suggests that human beings are "wired for God," that is, our genes have made belief in a transcendent reality as natural as our instincts.[3] Whether Benson is right or not, Christian faith proposes that the deepest order in human existence is our orientation toward God.

It is possible for humans to go against this orientation toward God and the First Commandment that articulates that order. In fact, the essence of sin is alienation from God. And God gives us room for that. We can live separated from God without falling to our death or being killed by lightning, even without suffering social penalties such as being socially outcast or put in prison. In fact, in some circles denial of God is socially encouraged. So it may seem as though people can manage very well without God. Nevertheless, Christian faith claims that human life is truly whole when we trust and love God above all else. God has created us that way.

God possesses spiritual rule. God's resistance to evil also tackles this deeper dimension of evil within the human heart. What is needed is a reorientation of a person's heart, so that he or she comes to trust and love God. Neither the expectations of social roles nor the ideals and demands of laws can accomplish that. What God seeks to do is win a person's trust and love by manifesting God's own trustworthiness and love for people. Here God works through the gospel, the good news of God's merciful grace in the life, death, and resurrection of Jesus Christ. Martin Luther calls this divine activity "God's spiritual kingdom or rule."

We can now pull together these several strands of thought and summarize Luther's vision of God's involvement in the stuff of daily life. His view is commonly called the doctrine of the two kingdoms. This doctrine distinguishes between God's worldly rule and God's spiritual rule. In the worldly kingdom, God as creator governs through law, including the expectations of constructive social roles. In the spiritual kingdom, God as redeemer governs through the gospel that changes the heart. Although these are usually called two kingdoms, they are not two different territories like Brazil and Venezuela, but two ways that God relates to people in this one world. There is a distinction but not a separation between the creative and redemptive modes of divine activity. Opposed to both God's worldly and spiritual rule, is the kingdom of the devil.[4]

In this vision God is very much involved in the stuff of daily life. On the one hand, God as creator continuously uses various persons, social roles, institutions, and laws to build up human life and to protect people from evil. Here God the creator acts within daily life through creaturely masks. On the other hand, God the redeemer is at work seeking to reorient the lives of persons from within by persuading them with love to trust the bountiful goodness of God. God is not far off, but near at hand.

CHRISTIAN VOCATION IN MARRIAGE AND WORK

Although persons who perform constructive functions are God's instruments of care for others, God calls believers to knowingly and willingly join in this divine work. Not only is there a divine summons to faith, then, but also a call of believers to service in the social roles of their daily life. Martin Luther's teaching about this call to service is named the "doctrine of vocation," for the word *vocation* comes from the Latin word for call.[5] While this is formulated as a doctrine, a set of ideas, its real thrust is to articulate the impact of the faith relationship with God on the everyday stuff of life such as marriage and work.

MARRIAGE

The doctrine of vocation challenges assumptions in the culture and invests the stuff of ordinary life with divine significance. For example, it is a common assumption in Western societies today that marriage is a conditional agreement between two individuals who define the agreement in terms of their mutual happiness. Frequently in the background is the conviction that an individual's highest purpose is to become the unique self that one "truly" is. Included in this notion is the belief that each individual has a unique potential waiting to be discovered and affirmed, and the path toward it is found through following one's feelings. This widespread conception of *self-realization* forms the moral framework within which marriage is often understood.[6] Marriage is one more means for self-realization in this sense of actualizing one's unique potential. If a marriage fails to deliver this, then it may legitimately be terminated.

Understanding marriage as a divine vocation puts things in a very different light. First, the popular notion of self-realization is called into question. The idea that our potential true self is just waiting to unfold is challenged by Jesus' words, "If any want to become my followers, let them deny themselves and take up their cross and follow me" (Mark 8:34). This suggests that Christian discipleship involves a break with one's former self. In a similar vein, Paul interprets the path to true identity as involving death of the old self and resurrection of a new self through God's grace. In other words, when one's relationship with Christ becomes the core of one's identity, the entire vision of one's true self is transformed. There is indeed a lifelong movement of discovering one's true self in Christ, but over time one becomes increasingly aware that this is a matter of being led by God to become more like Christ, rather than of autonomously doing whatever one wishes. Second, within this moral framework of divine vocation, marriage is viewed as a covenant before God with promises of lifelong fidelity to one another. Marriage is seen as a divine calling to serve the partner and any children that come. To be sure, human frailty and sin sometimes produce marriages that are miserable and even abusive, so there are situations when the best available option is divorce. Nonetheless, the basic understandings of self and marriage are shaped by the conviction that God not only loves and accepts the individual, but also calls that individual to serve spouse and perhaps children.

Underlying the idea of divine vocation is the faith relationship with God. As that faith relationship deepens, a person becomes more considerate of others. As we have seen, God's gracious presence both accepts and transforms. So in addition to the changes in understanding of self already mentioned, there is increased love for others. This is not just love as an ideal, a moral standard that tells us what we *ought* to be, although love always is that, too. This is also love as a motive, love in the heart that moves one to actually reach out. The closer one lives with the God of compassionate love, the more one naturally takes on that quality. Such compassionate love is immensely valuable for marriage, because the warm glow of romantic love fluctuates and two people living in close proximity year after year are bound to encounter disappointments, irritations, frustrations, and hurts. Patience, readiness to forgive, and the will to care for the partner who has perhaps become a burden are extremely valuable for sustaining a marriage. Christians do not have a corner on these qualities, by any means, yet a faith relationship with the gracious God is amazingly powerful in generating those wonderful qualities that Paul calls fruits of the Spirit, "love, joy, peace, patience, kindness, generosity, faithfulness, gentleness, and self-control" (Galatians 5:22-23). Thus Christian faith not only invests the marriage relationship with profound meaning, but also equips a person to live in that relationship with compassionate love.

WORK

Three purposes of work are widely acknowledged by religious and nonreligious folk.[7] First, work is a means for getting the things needed for living. Paid work earns the money to purchase food, clothing, and other necessities for oneself and maybe one's family. Unpaid housework prepares the food and washes the clothes. For some people, this is all there is to work: "It's just a job," or "It's just plain work." Without other meaning, though, work becomes a burden hard to bear over time. Second, work may also be a means of self-fulfillment. In this case, people put themselves into their work. The work elicits expression of their abilities and talents, and they feel satisfaction in doing it well. Third, many recognize work as a contribution to the common good. While this may be most obvious in human service areas such as nursing, others may also have a sense that their work in some way benefits people.

The Christian doctrine of vocation has several important implications for the meaning of work.

1. Those who perform work with low social status may have a sense of value and dignity in what they do. Societies tend to grade types of work. In the medieval European world, the special religious activities of monks, nuns, and priests were regarded as higher than the ordinary duties of changing diapers and plowing a field. Luther's teaching on vocation said that any kind of beneficial work was as noble in God's eyes as any other. In contemporary societies, physicians have high status and high pay, while those who do custodial or housework have low status and low pay or no pay. The doctrine of vocation encourages us to see equal dignity in all helpful forms of work.

2. Persons of faith who do not find their work personally fulfilling would recognize deeper significance to their work, for they would see themselves participating in God's care for the world by contributing to the good of others. Those who do custodial or housework may or may not enjoy their labor, but in either case they can take pride and satisfaction in knowing they perform an essential service.

3. For those who do find self-fulfillment in their work, living the doctrine of vocation dampens the tendency to invest *too much* significance in their work. For some people the temptation is to depend too much on their work for a sense of worth. Success at work

(including schoolwork) comes to mean too much. Unless one does well, one feels crushed and worthless. Then work has become an idol, a sort of god in which one seeks primary meaning and value. Living as one called to service by a gracious God, though, fundamentally changes the situation. On the one hand, satisfaction and pride gained from one's success pale beside the incomparable gifts of God. Increasingly, even abilities that enable one to succeed at work are humbly appreciated as God's gifts. On the other hand, failures become less trying, for one's identity and sense of value are less closely tied to personal performance.

Public Life

Our concern here with public life is roughly the same as what is often called "social ethics." All Christian ethics have a social and public dimension; nothing is purely personal and private. Yet in common usage, *social ethics* refers to those ethical issues related to large and complex social institutions—politics, economics, and culture. Involvement in these spheres is what I mean by public life. Of course, we already entered the social/public realm when we discussed marriage and work, both of which reflect culture, economic system, and political interests (e.g., "family values" in recent American politics), but with marriage and work we tend to have our eyes close to the ground of everyday life. Now we try to lift our eyes from the immediate round of day-to-day existence to consider Christian responsibility for wider issues in society, wider issues that may also impinge on family or work. For example, the issues of abortion, euthanasia, and peacemaking touch individuals, families, and civil law, while the issue of poverty relates also to work.

Individuals and Christian traditions have differed in their approach to social ethics. A classic study by the American ethicist H. Richard Niebuhr distinguished five major approaches to what he called "the Christ and culture issue."[8]

1. *Christ against culture.* Christian faith is viewed as fundamentally opposed to life in the political, economic, and cultural patterns of the larger society; hence, these Christians withdraw into their separate

society. The Amish exemplify this outlook, for most of them live apart in their own farming communities and do not use gasoline engines or serve in public office or the military.

2. *Christ of culture.* Christian faith is understood as smoothly compatible with contemporary ways in political, economic, and cultural life. This approach is not strictly identifiable with any denomination, but characterizes individuals and groups within numerous denominations. This can take liberal or conservative forms. The liberal sees Jesus as an example of a new movement, the conservative regards Jesus as embodiment of the old ways. They both accommodate Christian faith to their culture.

3. *Christ and culture in synthesis.* This stance has an appreciative attitude toward the political, economic, and cultural patterns of a society, but believes they need to be enriched and fulfilled through faith in Christ. There is a drive to bring about a creative synthesis. This has been characteristic of the Roman Catholic tradition, and the medieval synthesis of Christian faith with classical and European culture is one example.

4. *Christ and the conversion of culture.* This outlook begins with a deeper awareness of sin in human life than the previous view, yet believes that faith in Christ can bring about a conversion of persons and society. As the Reformed tradition has embodied this approach, it has tried to build a theocracy, a society governed by Scripture and Christian leaders. Historical examples are mid-sixteenth-century Geneva under John Calvin, mid-seventeenth-century England under Oliver Cromwell, and the Massachusetts Bay Colony in colonial America.

5. *Christ and culture in tension.* Those who follow this approach regard the political, economic, and cultural life of a society as highly ambiguous, that is, as a complex mix of good and evil. As part of God's ongoing creative activity, social institutions are positive means for sustaining and improving life on earth. But social practices and organizations, like the people who devise them, are also very vulnerable to

corruption. Thus there should be a continual tension between Christian faith and culture. This is the view favored by Augustine, Martin Luther, and most Lutherans. We have already encountered basic elements of this paradoxical approach in connection with marriage and work, and now we will examine its relevance for public life.

A dialectical relation is one that includes both yes and no, affirmation and negation. Martin Luther frequently made dialectical statements in his theology, not out of perversity or sloppy thinking, but because he believed God's ways of working in the world could best be expressed in them. The key dialectic or paradox for public life and social ethics is Luther's doctrine of two kingdoms, which is correlated with the dialectic of law and gospel. According to Luther, politics, economics, and culture, as well as family life, are means by which God continues to create and sustain the worldly realm. For instance, in the political sphere, local, regional, and national governments are masks by which God provides people with water, sewer, electricity, roads, schools, safety, settlement of disputes, and so forth. To the degree that governments carry out these responsibilities with justice, they fulfill the will of God for them. Although Luther and several generations of Lutherans after him thought of the political order and other so-called orders of creation as unchanging, this need not be so. Most contemporary Lutheran theologians recognize that social institutions change. Similarly, Luther often spoke especially of government in chiefly negative terms as a restraining force against chaos and evil, yet it is possible within the two kingdoms framework to think of government and other social orders as serving also positive functions. Perhaps, then, with some qualifications, the basic point holds, namely, that insofar as a particular social arrangement serves human well-being, it is an instrument through which the Creator works.

An integral element in the dialectical outlook is that evil is also powerfully and persistently present in the world. God's activity is opposed by evil—evil within human beings and also within social institutions including governments. This reading of the human situation runs counter to many other interpretations of public life that see evil in some areas of human experience but regard one area free from evil. There have been many such beliefs. On the one hand, some have viewed prevailing social institutions and beliefs as deeply flawed, but put confidence in a special social movement to bring about the truly good society. Modern scientific research, technological development, communism, fascism, socialism, feminism, and environmentalism are some of the movements on which high hopes have been pinned. These movements grasp varying degrees of truth and goodness, but some devoted followers go too far and believe their social movement will finally set things on the right course. On the other hand, many disillusioned by the events of modern history have lost confidence in all social movements and institutions. They place their trust in an unsullied potential deep within each individual. For some, that pure foundation is reason, for others free will, for still others our deepest feelings. Contrary to all such beliefs that look to something in society or the individual to put things right, the paradoxical perspective emphasizes that only God can finally make things right and bring salvation. Short of God ultimately making salvation complete, all we have are ambiguous circumstances, persons, institutions, and movements that are relatively better or worse.

Within this dialectical perspective, it is critical to distinguish what is relatively better from what is worse. While every person, institution, and movement is a mix of good and bad, it is important to support what brings a greater degree of justice. In practice, however, many Lutherans have not done this well. The principle fault of Lutheran social ethical practice has been to separate faith from public life. Personal faith and religious practice were often thought to belong to one sphere, while economic and political matters belonged to another sphere separate from faith. In other words, the *distinction* between the worldly and spiritual kingdoms frequently became a *separation*. Through the seventeenth, eighteenth, and nineteenth centuries, most Lutheran territories in Europe had a system in which the prince or king controlled the church as well as the state, and it was often accepted that the prince ran political and economic affairs according to principles quite separate from the convictions of Christian faith. In 1933 when Hitler sought to control the church, this tradition of deference to civil authority in all matters contributed to the fact that most German Lutherans supported the constitutionally chosen Hitler, although a minority such as Martin Niemoller and Dietrich Bonhoeffer bravely opposed him. In America, where religion has not faced domination by civil authorities, most Lutherans have only rather recently emerged from their ethnic enclaves; they have been slow to express the implications of their faith for political, economic, and cultural questions.

Since the end of World War II in 1945, many Lutherans have worked at making connections between Christian faith and public life. In Europe, a number of Lutheran churches established "Evangelical academies," which bring together representatives from various segments of society and church leaders to discuss major issues. For instance, the Evangelical academy at Loccum near Hanover, Germany, has sponsored conferences at which leaders from government, business, labor, medicine, law, and journalism meet with church leaders in both formal and informal settings to discuss major issues. The academy also funds a number of publications on these topics. On the whole, Lutheran churches have become more bold to speak out on public issues, sometimes through bishops and theologians, other times through official church statements.

An underlying question in all this has been the basic approach to social ethics. Because historically Lutherans have been rather poor at connecting Christian faith with the relative distinctions in public life, some Lutheran theologians today, like Larry Rasmussen, reject the two kingdoms framework itself. Rasmussen calls the church to three activist functions in society: critique of existing injustice; vision of better, even utopian, possibilities; and social pioneering or experimentation within the church itself. But most theologians support a revitalized two kingdoms ethic. In fact, Lutheran ethicist Robert Benne argues that the Lutheran "paradoxical vision" is very much needed as a corrective to utopian efforts both by religious groups to create the kingdom of God on earth and by secular groups to produce the ideal society.[9] This difference in orientation appears in statements on capital punishment by The Lutheran Church—Missouri Synod (LCMS) and the Evangelical Lutheran Church in America.

The Missouri Synod Commission on Theology and Church Relations in 1976 issued a "Report on Capital Punishment" that has four conclusions. (1) The primary conclusion of the report is, "Government has the right and authority to apply the death penalty." This point is grounded in Scripture (particularly Genesis 9:6 and Romans 12:19) and in the Lutheran confessions, especially Luther's comment in the Large Catechism that the Fifth Commandment, "You shall not kill," applies to individuals but not to governments. The report recognizes that some oppose capital punishment by invoking "Scriptural admonitions to Christian charity, compassion, and forgiveness" as well as Paul's injunction to leave vengeance to God (Romans 12:19). The report responds, "Inherent in this kind of argumentation is, at least in part, a failure to distinguish between God's kingdom of grace and His rule in power." Thus the two kingdoms doctrine is used to clearly affirm a government's authority to use the death penalty.

The report's remaining three conclusions qualify this authority. (2) "The authority of the government to apply the death penalty can be abused." The power is to be tempered by justice and in certain instances by charity (e.g., lighter punishment for accidental homicide than for premeditated homicide). While it is admitted that the death penalty has been imposed most often on persons of lower social status, considerably more attention is given to defenses against this criticism. (3) "Government is not required to exercise its right to administer the death penalty." This makes it possible for Lutherans to disagree over whether capital punishment should be actually used. (4) "Christians should exert a positive influence on the government's exercise of its responsibility of bearing the sword." While it is important to distinguish the two kingdoms, they should not be totally separated. The Christian should be like a man who is both a father and a policeman; the two roles are distinguished, yet one's relationship as father may at times influence what one does as policeman. For instance, out of compassion Christians should work to correct the spiritual, educational, economic, and social problems that contribute to crime.

In summary, the LCMS "Report on Capital Punishment" strongly affirms a government's right to have a death penalty for certain crimes. The questions of whether the death penalty has been an effective deterrent and been fairly applied are treated in such a manner that the arguments against the penalty on these grounds are neutralized. On balance, the report leans toward support of capital punishment, but leaves room for individual Lutherans to argue that government might better serve order and justice by employing another form of punishment. With some qualifications, Robert Benne approves the approach employed in this report, whereas Larry Rasmussen would likely criticize it for being too socially conservative and short on imagination of new, gospel-inspired possibilities for civil justice.

At the ELCA 1991 Churchwide Assembly, more than two-thirds of the delegates approved a social statement on the death penalty that opposes capital punishment. This statement reflects some of the debates among Lutherans about the two kingdoms approach to social ethics. On the one hand, the statement clearly expresses key elements of a two kingdoms ethic in this affirmation, "On the basis of Scripture and the Lutheran confessions we hold that, through the divine activity of the Law, God preserves creation, orders society, and promotes justice in a broken world. God works through the state and other structures of society necessary for life in the present age." So it endorses the idea that government and its law enforcement agencies are masks through which God works to preserve order in a sinful ("broken") world and that this activity belongs to the realm of law as distinguished from gospel. The statement admits, "God entrusts the state with power to take human life when failure to do so constitutes a clear danger to society." However, the emphasis is placed on alternatives.

The ELCA statement gives three reasons for opposing the death penalty. One is that the actual use of the death penalty is unjust, because race, gender, mental capacity, age, and affluence affect who is accused of murder and sentenced to death. Another reason is that capital punishment scapegoats individuals and ignores the whole society's responsibility for the root causes of violent crime. Both of these concerns about justice belong to the realm of law within a classic two kingdoms approach that distinguishes law and gospel.

The third reason for opposing capital punishment moves onto different ground when it says that following Jesus leads to restorative justice whereas capital punishment focuses on retribution. The entire system of legal penalties is based on the notion of *retributive justice*, that is, justice is done when a person who has caused harm to another has to endure a balancing penalty. Exact retributive justice would be an eye for an eye; in other words, a punishment equal to the injury. Although many societies have worked out a system of other compensatory punishments such as fines and imprisonment, capital punishment calls for an equivalent penalty, a life for a life. Instead of retributive justice, though, the ELCA statement calls for *restorative justice* that aims at rebuilding individual lives and human relationships. Restorative justice would try to heal and transform persons and families wounded by violence. For this idea of restorative strategy, the statement gives this rationale:

> Lutheran theological tradition has maintained that society is ruled by the Law and is influenced and nourished by the Gospel. Renewed by the Gospel, Christians, as salt of the earth (Matthew 5:13) and light of the world (Matthew 5:14), are called to respond to violent crime in the restorative way taught by Jesus (Matthew 5:38-39) and shown by his actions (John 8:3-11).

Inspiration for practicing restorative justice is drawn from the gospel and from moral instruction of Jesus that the Lutheran tradition has generally applied to Christians, but not to the wider society. In Matthew 5:38-39, Jesus tells his disciples not to resist evil and to turn the other cheek, and in John 8:3-11 he tells a crowd of men ready to stone a woman caught in adultery that he who is without sin should cast the first stone. The ELCA statement says that society as a whole is "influenced and nourished by the Gospel." So restorative justice is not only something Christians should carry out in their own lives and ministry, but it should be reflected in the whole society's law governing violent crimes. This procedure would be praised by Larry Rasmussen as an example of the church using its Gospel-centered faith to envision a better possibility, but Robert Benne considers it a dubious move that confuses God's rule by grace with divine rule by law.[10]

A second question underlying Lutheran thought and action in social ethics is, How should the church make the influence of its faith felt in public life? Robert Benne argues that the primary means should be what he calls "indirect connections." These connections happen through Christian individuals and associations, but the church as an institution does not get directly involved. Many of these indirect connections happen without plan; as individuals are nurtured in the church, they tend to affirm beliefs and values that are reflected in their views and activities related to political, economic, and cultural issues. But sometimes the church also intends to establish indirect connections with public life. The European evangelical academies are good examples, for there the church sponsors discussions between church members and leaders in society without endorsing a particular position. Other examples are church-sponsored efforts at social pioneering such as establishing hospitals, hospices, orphanages, homes for the elderly, and colleges. Sometimes individual Christians will also form a voluntary association like Bread for the World to pursue a cause that the church as an institution does not directly support. Larry Rasmussen also endorses these indirect connections, but gives greater prominence to the intentional church efforts. He especially encourages social pioneering by Christian voluntary associations.

Another means by which Lutheran churches sometimes influence public life is through *direct connections,* where the church as an institution speaks or acts. The Missouri Synod and ELCA statements on the death penalty are instances of a church as an institution speaking out on an issue in public life. Although both these statements endorse a certain stance on capital punishment, they also explicitly acknowledge that church members may hold a different position on some points. In some cases, Lutheran churches go beyond expression of a moral position to action that tries to shape public policy and legislation accordingly. For example, the LCMS has engaged in public advocacy for changing the legal status of abortion in the United States, and the ELCA has been even more aggressive by establishing Offices for Governmental Affairs in Washington, New York, and a number of state capitols for the purpose of advocacy.[11]

Should the church be involved in these direct connections? Both Benne and Rasmussen heartily support the church speaking out on pertinent public issues, although Benne is more cautious about how it is done. He warns that the church should speak out relatively infrequently and should affirm ethical principles without backing specific proposals for ordering society. Benne is still more cautious about the church engaging in advocacy, although he believes the church should do so on occasion. His recommendation is that the church should advocate in cases of great evil or great good, but should avoid advocacy in the vast middle ground. Here, too, the church should concentrate on calling attention to a problem without prescribing a particular solution.

On the whole, Rasmussen favors a very active role for the church on social issues. Besides speaking out and advocacy, the institutional church should encourage social pioneering both within its own organization and by voluntary associations allied with it. For instance, the church should seek to embody an inclusive vision such as the ELCA's commitment to multiculturalism, with its quota system of representation to boards and assemblies. There should be many experiments, some of which will take prudent, gradual form, while others will take daring, utopian form. He admits that it is difficult for such diversity to coexist in the church, but believes that is needed. All in all, Benne and Rasmussen agree that it is vital for the church to take seriously political, economic, and cultural issues, but they exhibit some significant differences in how to go about it. Their agreements and differences are suggestive of an even wider spectrum of opinion among Lutherans generally about the relevance of Christian faith for public life.

In this chapter, we have been considering the dimension of service in Lutheran spirituality. Whereas some Christian traditions have focused on a special form of religious life shaped by celibacy, poverty, and obedience to proper authority, Lutheran spirituality has always been a faith thoroughly enmeshed in the stuff of ordinary life. According to Luther's two kingdoms perspective, God is intimately present in social existence, although present in two modes—as creator, who sustains and builds up human life through bonds of obligation and mutual care, and as redeemer, who reconciles and transforms persons through generous love. In this dialectical outlook, the Christian is called by God to serve others in and through the relationships and responsibilities of daily life. We have highlighted vocation to service in marriage and family, work, and public life, although there is also service in friendship, neighborhood, and church. Faith in divine vocation describes a relationship with God that invests ordinary existence with profound meaning and fuels one's existence with the virtues allied with compassionate love. This faith's orientation to service reaches into all spheres of public life, but there are differences among contemporary Lutherans over how Christian faith and especially the institutional church should be related to public life. Some, like Robert Benne, believe there should be a clear distinction between the gospel message of salvation and efforts at making society relatively more just; related to this is the belief that the church should concentrate on proclaiming the gospel and rather infrequently speak and rarely act as an institution on disputed political, economic, or cultural questions. Others believe that the gospel message may inspire better ways in which a society may order aspects of its common life, such as endeavors in restorative justice within the penal system. Among these, some incorporate this emphasis within a two-kingdom framework; some like Larry Rasmussen employ an alternative ethical scheme. The debate is ongoing, and the issues are important.

FOR REFLECTION AND PRACTICE

1. In what areas of your life do you have a sense of service? How is God, if at all, connected with this service?

2. What is your attitude toward the various kinds of work you do? (Remember that work is not necessarily paid labor, so a student, housewife, househusband, or retired person also works.) Does the doctrine of vocation have anything to add to your convictions about work?

3. In regard to the death penalty, with which of the two Lutheran statements on this question do you agree more? Why?

4. Do you think a Lutheran church should issue statements on disputed moral questions in society such as the death penalty? Why?

5. What does your congregation do to foster moral responsibility on social ethical issues? Should it do more or less? Why?

6. Meditate for ten to fifteen minutes on Matthew 25:31-46. Afterward ask yourself what the implications of this passage are for you personally and for the church.

9

TAKING STOCK

WE HAVE THE OPPORTUNITY AND RESPONSIBILITY TO affirm a faith to guide our life. We do this by connecting our life story with a Big Story, which sets forth a view of reality and the wider significance of human life. We have been reflecting on the Christian story. The Christian story is a Big Story that comes in different versions. The New Testament already includes various versions, for Matthew, Mark, Luke, John, Paul, Peter, James, and others tell the Christian story in somewhat different fashion. To be sure, there is much in common, for they all proclaim Jesus as God's Messiah. Nevertheless, each tells the story with his own accent. So it is also with later Christian leaders and communities. Each denomination has its own rendition of the Christian story.

We have been considering the Lutheran version of the Christian story. When we look closer, of course, we find that the Lutheran version itself has variations within it. To name just a few, there are evangelical Lutherans and charismatic Lutherans, evangelical catholic Lutherans and fundamentalist Lutherans, Japanese Lutherans and African American Lutherans. Lutheran Christians are a recognizable family whose members bear a resemblance to one another without being identical. The same is true of other major Christian spiritual traditions. In this chapter, I would like us to take stock of the Lutheran spiritual tradition and ask what part, if any, that tradition might play in our own spiritual life.

We have been considering Lutheran Christianity as a spirituality. I have said a spirituality is comprised of a lived faith plus a path. Of course, faith includes a set of beliefs, a theology, but a lived faith is always more than a set of ideas. A lived faith involves giving oneself to something (commitment) and also trust in something. A spirituality also means a path, a set of practices whose aim is to nurture faith and to give expression to that faith. What we have done in previous chapters is to examine the beliefs and commitments of faith in the Lutheran tradition, and the fundamental forms and practices intended to feed and manifest that faith.

Our consideration of Lutheran spirituality is taking place within a cultural era when there is renewed attention to spiritual practices. As we noted earlier, Princeton sociologist Robert Wuthnow says that in the United States (I believe it is also true of most Western societies), we have come through a time of much seeking that has often resulted in spiritual dabbling. He suggests what is needed now is a spirituality of practice that may employ various practices, yet is firmly grounded in a solid spiritual tradition that lends coherence and depth. Our question now is whether Lutheran spirituality might be that solid spiritual tradition or a major contributor to it. With this deeply existential question in mind, we want to take stock of Lutheran spirituality.

As we step back to assess this tradition, we shall do four things: (1) review the main features of Lutheran spirituality by taking a fresh look at it from a different perspective, (2) briefly compare Lutheran spirituality with two other Christian spiritual traditions, (3) recognize some shortcomings of the Lutheran tradition, and (4) identify the strengths or gifts that Lutheran spirituality offers individuals and the whole church.

Review of Lutheran Spirituality

Viewing something from a fresh perspective often helps us understand it better, so now we will review Lutheran spirituality from the perspective of Ninian Smart, a comparative religions scholar. Smart says religions and nonreligious worldviews typically have seven dimensions: experience, story, doctrine, rituals and practices, physical symbols, ethics, and social organization.[1] Looking at these seven dimensions in Lutheran spirituality will enrich our understanding.

1. *Experience.* Experience is concrete and specific to each tradition and person, yet Smart says there are two broad types of religious

experience: experience of a personal God and mystical/contemplative experience. In *experience of a personal God*, people interact with God somewhat like meeting another human person. For instance, in Exodus 3, Moses encounters God through a burning bush as a disembodied voice calls him to deliver the Israelites from their slavery in Egypt. Interacting with the personal God through words and visible symbols has been the predominant form of religious experience in Christianity and in Lutheranism.

Various traditions within Christianity have highlighted different experiences of the personal God. In Lutheran spirituality, the particular religious experience that has been emphasized is personal knowledge of God's merciful grace. Here God is experienced as a loving God who freely accepts and empowers a person. The relationship with God is felt to be rather like a relationship between two human persons, except that God is infinite.

Less common in Christianity has been *contemplative or mystical experience* in which the emphasis is on awareness of the divine presence. In some forms of contemplative experience, the divine is known more in silence as a mysterious presence beyond all words and symbols. Christian communities that especially value this experience often establish places apart from ordinary life such as monasteries, in order to provide ample silence and solitude. This sort of mystical involvement has not been common among Lutherans who stress engagement in ordinary life.

Other forms of contemplative experience are closer to the first broad type of religious experience—interaction with the personal God—for in these mystical experiences God is known as a personal presence. The apostle Paul speaks of this when he says, "It is no longer I who live, but it is Christ who lives in me" (Galatians 2:20). Martin Luther and a number of others in the Lutheran tradition have cherished this Pauline form of contemplative experience of the present Christ.

Since human experience is affected by many factors such as time, place, culture, and life events, there has always been diversity in religious or spiritual experience among Lutherans. Nevertheless, the central experience generally encouraged and valued within the Lutheran tradition has been experience of God's merciful grace, the experience of God's unconditional acceptance and transforming power.

2. *Word or story.* For Christians, this is the Big Story of the Bible that communicates a comprehensive vision of life and reality. In common with other Protestants, Lutherans regard the word as the primary means of grace. In their worship services, reading, preaching, and singing, the word of God takes pride of place. In their educational programs, study of Scripture is fundamental. In their everyday existence, they are encouraged to read and meditate on the Bible. Among Lutherans the Christian Big Story is communicated primarily through words that tell of God's revelation in Israel and Jesus. The heart of this Big Story for Lutherans is the gospel, the good news of God's grace in Jesus Christ. To that gospel they return again and again like bees to honey.

3. *Sacraments and physical symbols.* According to Smart, religions have a material dimension, for their worldview is manifested in physical symbols such as sacraments, visual art, architecture, and sacred places. He points out that religious traditions vary greatly in the prominence given to physical symbols. He cites, on the one hand, Calvinist Christianity (Reformed) as a movement that has shunned material symbols, and on the other hand, Orthodox Christianity as a community rich in material symbols. While there are variations within the Lutheran family, generally Lutheran spirituality has placed moderate emphasis on the material. The sacraments of baptism and the Lord's supper have considerable prominence among Lutherans, and material symbols are generally quite evident in their church buildings.

4. *Rituals and practices.* Smart makes a rough distinction between rituals as more formal and practices as less formal. For instance, mass celebrated by the pope is usually a highly elaborate ritual, whereas yoga in Hindu tradition is a practice intended to heighten spiritual awareness. In either case, ritual and practice are patterned behaviors that nurture and express the faith of a particular religion or spirituality. All religions have some rituals and practices, and so do all Christian traditions.

Christian traditions vary on what specific rituals and practices they follow and on the degree of formality or informality. Most Lutheran churches use the ritual of the Western rite liturgy for at least some of their worship services, while some also use patterns from older revivalist movements or the charismatic movement or contemporary church growth movement. In fact, larger Lutheran congregations often try to accommodate different degrees of formality and informality with a menu of different worship services. Sometimes a practice can become controversial; this has been the case with speaking in tongues among Lutherans, so rules governing tongues have often been adopted at the congregational and denominational levels.

5. *Doctrine.* Smart points out that in addition to stories, religious/spiritual worldviews commonly also have doctrines or formal teachings. Whereas a story conveys a message through narrative, a doctrine is a more abstract intellectual formulation. In some religious traditions, doctrine is very important, in others it is insignificant. In Christianity, while the Bible consists in good part of narrative, it also includes some doctrines such as Paul's teaching on justification. In subsequent centuries, the ancient church adopted several creeds to address disputed questions, and churches generally have also approved at least some formal doctrines to express their beliefs. Nevertheless, Christian traditions differ appreciably in the weight and attention given to doctrine. The Lutheran tradition is one that places a high value on Christian doctrine articulated in the classic creeds and in the Lutheran confessions.

6. *Ethics.* Smart shows that religions have an ethical dimension, although they differ substantially on the extent to which this gets expressed in laws. For instance, in addition to the Ten Commandments, Judaism has over six hundred rules that the Orthodox Jew observes, and Islamic life has traditionally been governed by Islamic law, *sharia.* Other religious traditions are less tied to law, yet emphasize ethical principles. We have seen that the Lutheran tradition has a well-developed ethical perspective in which the ideas of God's twofold rule and vocation have been central, but there has been a special sensitivity to the danger of legalism.

7. *Social or institutional dimension.* Although anti-institutional feelings run high among many people today, humans are social beings. Spirituality also takes on some sort of social embodiment, whether in a small group that meets periodically, a retreat center with

its staff, a congregation, a movement with leadership of a fluid group of people, or a denomination.

Sometimes a religious/spiritual worldview is *the* view of an entire society. This has been the case generally with tribal religions. In medieval Europe, Christianity was the official religion. Many Lutheran territories after the Reformation shared a similar situation. Even though Lutherans claimed a theology that emphasized church as a community of believers created by Word and Sacrament, the actual social status of most Lutheran churches in Europe has been that of a favored territorial institution. Elsewhere, and surely in North America, Lutheranism has existed as one Christian denomination among many.

The internal social structure of Lutheran churches, both on the congregational and broader levels, has largely reflected the social structure of the society in which they exist. So in very hierarchical societies of seventeenth century Europe, the church was organized hierarchically. In African countries today, with traditions of strong tribal leaders Lutheran bishops are powerful figures in church life. In North America, where democratic ways are influential, Lutheran churches have made various accommodations between traditional church structure with bishops and democratic organization.

These seven dimensions of religion or spirituality are interwoven in Lutheran spirituality. For instance, a Lutheran understanding of the human predicament (see chapter 2) is part of the background for the central experience of God's merciful grace. This view of the human predicament is expressed in a ritual of confession and absolution common in Lutheran worship services as well as in doctrinal statements on sin and human freedom.

COMPARISON OF CHRISTIAN SPIRITUALITIES

Our understanding of Lutheran spirituality is also sharpened by comparing it with other Christian traditions. I will do this by using Smart's seven dimensions of religion/spirituality in thumbnail sketches of two other Christian traditions: Baptist and Roman Catholic. Each of these traditions is also a diverse family, but I will hazard brief descriptions that call attention to the most salient points without doing justice to that diversity. Comparison of the three traditions in spirituality is summarized in the chart on the next page.

Dimensions of Spirituality	Baptist	Roman Catholic	Lutheran
EXPERIENCE 1. Interactions with personal God	Stress conversion to faith in personal God	Stress spiritual growth through devotion to personal God	Stress merciful grace of personal God
2. Contemplative/mystical experience of God	Paul's "in Christ" mysticism subordinate	Mystical experience and the contemplative way highly valued	Paul's "in Christ" mysticism subordinate
WORD/BIBLICAL STORY	Primary means of grace: Bible, proclamation, songs	Secondary yet important means of grace	Primary means of grace: Bible, proclamation, hymns
SACRAMENTS AND PHYSICAL SYMBOLS	Two sacraments less prominent; few visual symbols	Seven sacraments primary means of grace; Many visible symbols	Two sacraments secondary, yet important; moderate use of visible symbols
RITUALS AND PRACTICES	Mostly revivalistic worship patterns; some Reformed patterns	Western rite liturgy and many other rituals	Western rite liturgy; free to use other worship forms
	Free prayer; Bible study and meditation	Wide variety of meditation and contemplative practices; devotion to Mary and Saints	Many written prayers; Bible study and meditation
DOCTRINE	Stress teachings of Bible; avoid creeds	Strong emphasis on classic creeds and Catholic doctrine	Strong emphasis on classic creeds and Lutheran confessions
ETHICS	Several ethical approaches	Synthesis of culture and Christian faith	Dialectical relation of culture and Christian faith
SOCIAL ORGANIZATION	Highly independent congregations associated in a conference	Pope/Council, Bishop and Diocese, parish; religious orders	Churchwide assembly, synod, and Bishop Congregation

1. Baptist spirituality has its center in religious *experiences* of interacting with the personal God. While experiences of growth in faith are not neglected, Baptists have focused more than most Christians on the conversion experience in which an individual makes his or her personal response of faith in Jesus Christ. Contemplation has not been encouraged. Attention to *word and biblical story* is fundamental; not only is there a strong emphasis on preaching and daily reading of the biblical word, but the Bible is regarded as the highest authority in all matters of faith. *Sacraments* (preferably called "ordinances") and *material* symbols generally are minimized; the eucharist is celebrated monthly or less often, and Baptist sanctuaries tend to have few visual symbols. Baptist *rituals and practices* reflect this emphasis on the conversion experience, for common elements are preaching—in good part oriented to conversion—and the revival meeting explicitly aimed at conversions. Well-known examples are Billy Graham's crusades, which invite people to make a decision for Christ. *Doctrine* is not unimportant, but many Baptists say the Bible is their expression of doctrine. Creeds are not commonly used in the worship service and official doctrinal statements are few. Walter Rauschenbusch is the only Baptist who comes close to being renowned as a theologian. What Baptists have produced are great preachers like Harry Emerson Fosdick, evangelists like Billy Graham, and some leaders in social justice like Rauschenbusch and Martin Luther King Jr. In *ethics* Baptists look to the Bible, have been strong advocates of religious freedom, and have the ethical teachings of Rauschenbusch and King, yet there is no generally recognized tradition of "Baptist ethics."[2] In *social organization* Baptists stress the independence of the local congregation; there are associations of congregations such as the Southern Baptist Convention. A common thread running through Baptist spirituality is an emphasis on voluntary participation that is manifest in the distinct conversion experience, the use of free prayer rather than written prayers, becoming a member of the church through the personal choice of baptism, and independence of the congregation.[3]

2. While it is hazardous to sketch Baptist spirituality in a few broad strokes, it is even more risky to attempt to do so with Roman Catholic spirituality, for with its longer history and nearly one billion members, it embraces such great diversity. Nevertheless, I think

a rough shape to Roman Catholic spirituality can be perceived. First of all, Roman Catholic spirituality is *sacramental*, for here faith is formed and fed primarily through the material dimension of the seven sacraments. Physical symbols are also prominent in sculpture, images, and elaborate dress for the priest during mass. Although the clergy and members of Catholic religious orders have long had extensive involvement with the biblical *word and story* through their daily offices of prayer, until recently the laity gained access to selected elements of the biblical story chiefly through rituals, devotional practices such as the rosary, and visual representations. Exposure to the word of God through preaching, devotional reading of the Bible, and song has been relatively weak for most Catholics, although the leadership is working to strengthen those areas. Attendance at the *ritual* of the mass with its Western rite liturgy revitalized at the Second Vatican Council (1962–65) is still basic, although mass attendance has relaxed considerably from pre–Vatican II days. Roman Catholicism has included a wide variety of spiritual *practices*, but one focal point that contributes significantly to Catholic identity vis-à-vis Protestant traditions and non-Christian religions is devotion to Mary and Christian saints.[4] Catholicism has encouraged both *experiences* of devotion to the personal God and contemplation, yet within both the devotional and contemplative, the Catholic emphasis has fallen on the experience of ongoing growth and transformation by grace. Talk of conversion among Catholics commonly refers to a continuing process rather than the distinct turning point event about which Baptists speak. *Doctrine* has been strongly emphasized in Roman Catholicism, so creeds, other authoritative teachings of the hierarchy, and theology have had a strong reciprocal relationship with various forms of its spirituality. In *ethics* Roman Catholicism has a long, rich tradition of moral theology. Its most distinctive feature has been an insistence on finding a synthesis of faith and reason, divine grace and human nature, faith and works.[5] *Social organization* with bishops and the pope has also been important, for Catholic consciousness is shaped significantly by awareness—in agreement or disagreement—of the church's hierarchy. Although this has diminished, many Roman Catholics feel theirs is most truly the church.

3. A similar sketch of Lutheran spirituality and comparison with the other two traditions will help us get a broad overview of its character as a tradition that falls between the Roman Catholic and Baptist ways. Some have spoken of this in-between status of Lutheranism by calling it a conservative reformation movement; others use the term *evangelical catholic.*

The evangelical, gospel-centered nature of Lutheran spirituality is evident in its primary focus on the *experience* of God's merciful grace, the grace that accepts the sinner. This experience belongs squarely in the realm of encounter with the personal God, although frequently, as in the apostle Paul, there are also elements of a personalized mysticism that focus on the presence of Christ in the believer. All this has its roots in Martin Luther's own experience that focused on the search for a merciful God. To be sure, Lutheran spirituality also involves the transforming grace of God. These two aspects of grace cannot be separated, for grace is not a thing, but God's way of relating to people through Christ. What Luther and most Lutherans emphasize in this relationship is the side of God's full acceptance and love of the sinner. Although there have been periodic pietist efforts to highlight the transformative side of the relationship with God, the primary experience in the tradition has been of God's merciful grace.

This focus on the experience of divine mercy distinguishes Lutheran spirituality from the other two forms of spirituality. Baptist spirituality is most akin to some forms of Lutheran pietism and contemporary Lutheran evangelicalism in their shared encouragement of a discrete conversion experience, yet these variant forms of Lutheran spirituality become more typically Lutheran insofar as the element of divine acceptance gains prominence. Most forms of Lutheran spirituality emphasize long term formation of faith within the church, rather than a turning-point decision. Yet the Lutheran family includes many for whom a distinct, memorable conversion is a significant part of their religious experience.

Roman Catholic spirituality places the main accent on experiences of growth or sanctification. The difference in the Roman Catholic and Lutheran traditions is evident, for example, in the turning-point experiences of Saint Ignatius Loyola, founder of the Catholic order of

Jesuits, and Martin Luther. While Ignatius was attracted by daydreams about performing heroic acts of service to the Lord as Saint Francis, Saint Dominic, and other saints had done, Luther was searching for a God who would accept him. In the end, Ignatius also discovered the merciful love of God and Luther also found the transforming power of the Spirit, yet the focal point of their religious experience was different.

In Word and Sacrament, the Lutheran family of spirituality occupies a mediating position between Roman Catholic and other Protestant traditions. When we compare our three spiritual traditions on their attention to *word and biblical story,* Lutherans and Baptists share a Protestant valuation of primary accentuation on the word. Preaching, reading, and studying the word are strongly emphasized in both. Singing the word is also very important in both communities, although what is sung in each is strongly influenced by different ethnic backgrounds and musical traditions. The hymns of a typical white Lutheran congregation will sound heavy to white Baptist ears, while what a typical white Baptist congregation sings will sound like camp songs to Lutheran ears. An African American Lutheran congregation will likely sing a blend of musical forms. A distinguishing mark of the Lutheran musical tradition is that it has both a large body of great art music as well as congregational music. In Roman Catholic spirituality, word takes second place to sacrament, and parish singing is often weak.

Among Lutherans *sacraments and physical symbols* are less prominent than with Catholics, but much more prominent than Baptists. Currently Lutherans celebrate the eucharist more often than Baptists, but less often than Roman Catholics. Similarly Lutherans generally fall between the other two traditions in regard to the number of symbols in their churches.

This mediating position of Lutheranism between Roman Catholicism and other Protestant churches is also apparent in *ritual and practices.* On the one hand, most Lutheran churches use a form of the Western rite liturgy very similar to the Roman Catholic mass. On the other hand, the pietistic strain in Lutheranism has favored worship patterns more akin to Baptist ways. In spiritual practices, Lutherans have been like other Protestants in their rejection of prayers to Mary and other saints, and their heavy reliance on prayer and meditation with Scripture or books based in Scripture. Lutherans have also shown considerable suspicion of the world detachment and religious disciplines frequently associated in Catholicism with the quest for contemplative experience. Yet many Lutherans, past and present, have drawn freely on Catholic sources for help in spiritual practices such as prayer, spiritual direction, retreat, and private confession.

When it comes to *doctrine*, Lutheran spirituality is very much like Roman Catholic spirituality in having a strong doctrinal component and heritage. Both communities firmly endorse the classic Christian creeds, have a rich body of confessions that help define their tradition, and make confession of a classic creed a regular part of their worship rituals. Nevertheless, there are some significant differences in the specific teachings the two churches hold. For example, Lutherans say that the doctrine of justification means Christians are righteous and sinners at the same time, whereas Roman Catholic teaching has serious reservations about that.[6] Of course, few lay Lutherans and Catholics are aware of the fine points of doctrine in their traditions, yet the emphasis on doctrine in their respective traditions means there is a definite cognitive content that is claimed to be true. The stress on doctrine tends to lend a specific shape to the rituals, practices, and community life that form spiritualities in each tradition. In both the clergy are required to be well educated, and a high respect for theological learning has produced some great theologians who have engaged the intellectual challenges of the modern era.

In the Baptist tradition today, the doctrine of Scripture is certainly a major matter of dispute, yet overall among Baptists, doctrines and confessions do not play such a prominent role either in the education of clergy or in customary worship and practices. The difference is evident in the fact that confession of a creed is a normal element in Lutheran and Roman Catholic worship, whereas use of a creed is unusual in Baptist worship. Among Baptists there is a strong restorationist spirit, that is, the conviction that they are returning to the beliefs and practices of the New Testament church. In a tradition that regularly uses a post-biblical creed, members are formed with a more explicit consciousness of participating in a community whose beliefs have also been shaped by a long historical process after the New Testament beginnings.

In *ethics* Lutherans have emphasized Christian service to others in and through the ordinary social roles and relationships of life. Whereas Roman Catholicism has for centuries held up life in various forms of celibate community as the ideal and only recently placed equally high value on lay spirituality, Lutheran spirituality has been a lay spirituality from the beginning. In this respect, Lutheran spirituality has much in common with fellow Protestants such as the Baptists, although the Lutheran view is distinguished from other Protestant ethical perspectives by its grounding in Luther's dialectical understanding of God's two kingdoms.

In respect to *social organization,* Lutheran churches take a stance between the Baptist and Roman Catholic traditions. Lutherans generally have less congregational autonomy than Baptists and more than Catholics. Unlike Baptists, Lutheran churches around the world generally have bishops, although they may be called district presidents or superintendents; however, the bishop's power is more limited than in Roman Catholicism. For Lutherans there is less attention to the whole question of obedience to hierarchical church authority on both jurisdictional and doctrinal matters that is an element in the Roman Catholic family of spirituality. Today there is considerable diversity of attitudes toward church authority among Roman Catholics, but it is an issue with which they all wrestle. Among Lutherans, first Scripture and then the Lutheran confessions have the highest authority, but frequently there is debate about how these authorities should be interpreted in regard to specific contemporary issues. Position statements approved by bishops or church assembly are not intended to have the same weight in forming the conscience of Lutherans as papal encyclicals are intended to have for Catholics. For instance, the ELCA statement on abortion is offered as "guidance" for its members. When it comes to the general ministry of the laity, a full-bodied Lutheran spirituality includes the priesthood of all believers in which believers pray for others and teach them divine things. At present, though, this is a potential waiting to be more fully actualized.

This comparison of Lutheran spirituality with Baptist and Roman Catholic spirituality underscores the character of Lutheran spirituality as an evangelical catholic family of spirituality. Some Lutherans lean more toward the evangelical side, others more toward the

catholic side. As a total family, though, Lutherans manifest characteristics of both.

SHORTCOMINGS OF THE LUTHERAN TRADITION

Like every other human creation, the Lutheran spiritual tradition has
flaws. Part of being true to this spirituality, which takes sin very seriously, is to acknowledge its own shortcomings. Without claiming to
be exhaustive, I shall call attention to three deficiencies.

One major fault of Lutheranism is that it has been predominantly
oriented toward males. Along with most other religious communities
in the world, Lutheran churches have been patriarchal. Until rather
recently in Lutheran churches, only men served as clergy and members of most congregational and synodical boards. Indeed, aside
from the women's organizations, the institutional history of
Lutheranism has been written with little mention of women. Lutheran churches have also been male-centered in their language and
thought patterns. Some churches, including The Lutheran Church—
Missouri Synod and Wisconsin Evangelical Lutheran Synod, hold
that Scripture (especially 2 Corinthians 11; 1 Corinthians 14; and 1
Timothy 2) teaches a subordination of women to men and allows
only men to fill the pastoral functions of public worship.[7] Although
ordination of women was approved by most European Lutheran
churches and, in 1970, by the main predecessor bodies of the Evangelical Lutheran Church in America, patriarchal patterns in language,
behavior, and organization are quite persistent in those churches as
well. Some women feel so left out of Lutheran churches that they
look elsewhere for a more welcoming spiritual community. An
important task for Lutherans is to establish a faith and practice that
is hospitable to both women and men.

A second weakness of the Lutheran tradition is that it has been so
Eurocentric, that is, its membership and dominant culture has been
strongly northern European. Of the approximately 61 million
Lutherans are in the world, 61 percent are in European churches and
14 percent in North American churches, which are heavily northern
European in composition. In addition, a significant proportion of
Lutherans in Latin America and Australia are of European heritage.

Again, Lutheranism is not alone among Christian churches in being ethnocentric, yet the fact that it is a widely shared problem does not eliminate the drawback. Part of the difficulty is that so many of those who are counted as Lutherans in Europe are merely nominal members. Another part of the problem is that Lutheranism's close ties to European or white American culture have made it less than inviting to people from other cultures. One of the main challenges facing the Lutheran spiritual tradition today is whether it can adapt to a variety of cultures while preserving its core gospel-centered identity.

A third, related flaw is that Lutherans have been uneven in their evangelism. In Scandinavia and many parts of Germany, the experience of being in a dominant, state-supported Lutheran church left its mark on generations of Lutherans; many were Lutherans by default. To be sure, Lutheran pietism spawned mission efforts both at home and abroad. A number of mission societies were formed in the eighteenth and nineteenth centuries to support the work in German and Scandinavian colonies and elsewhere. While today evangelism is a high priority among most Lutherans in developing nations, for the majority of Western Lutherans it is not. Old patterns of hesitancy about witnessing to the Christian faith are reinforced in the contemporary pluralistic situation by reluctance to intrude on what is widely regarded as another person's purely private choice of faith. This lack of missionary drive does not lend itself well to meeting the challenges of a pluralistic society in which loyalty to any church, much less a particular denomination, is not a given. This weakness coupled with the Eurocentric character of the tradition threaten to make Lutheran faith the spirituality of an ever declining community.

No spiritual tradition comes without flaws. For some people, these Lutheran shortcomings and others may be so great as to severely limit the desire to draw sustenance from this tradition. For others the tradition may offer enough strengths to make it a source of spiritual vitality. It is to those strengths that we now turn.

Special Gifts of Lutheran Spirituality

Paul likens the church to the human body. Just as the body has a diversity of parts, each of which contributes to the functioning of the whole, so the Holy Spirit gives a variety of gifts (in Greek, *charisms*) to different members of the church (1 Corinthians 12). Building on this, the Second Vatican Council urged the many Roman Catholic religious orders to examine anew their founders and history, in order to identify and revitalize the *charism(s)* that the Holy Spirit had given their order for the upbuilding of the church. I propose that something similar should be done by Lutherans and Christians in other traditions.

For example, the brief description of Baptist spirituality suggests that one of its mighty *charisms*, much needed in today's world, is the passion for personal evangelism that stresses explicit witness to Jesus Christ. Among the *charisms* of Roman Catholic spirituality are its powerful sacramentalism, closely related rich appreciation of gesture and material symbols in ritual, its religious orders, and the papacy.

All these traditions and gifts do not fit neatly together to create a community whose members all agree with one another. For instance, Protestants and Catholics generally have major disagreements over the papacy. However, as a Lutheran I regard the papacy as a gift meant for the whole church, and I hope one day Christians of many traditions may agree sufficiently upon a revised form of papal ministry as an instrument of unity and witness. In the meantime, the Roman Catholic Church is the primary caretaker of the papal *charism*. So it goes with a number of *charisms* borne by specific Christian traditions.

It was not much different in the early church. To be sure, the early church over time rejected some beliefs as inconsistent with faith in Jesus Christ, but the range of views in the New Testament writings testifies to considerable diversity within the Christian community. For example, Paul and James sang the Christian song in substantially different ways, yet they both were included in the same choir. Today also we should expect a variety of voices in the Christian choir, each voice with its own strength and beauty to contribute. So what are the *charisms* that Lutheran spirituality bears?

1. One Lutheran *charism* is its strong doctrinal heritage, especially the Lutheran confessions and other writings of Martin Luther. Luther is one of the very greatest of Christian theologians, ranking with

Augustine, Aquinas, and Calvin. Naturally, Luther does not belong only to Lutherans, no more than Aquinas belongs only to Roman Catholics or to Aquinas' own religious order of Dominicans. Nevertheless, just as Dominicans take it as their special responsibility to study Thomas Aquinas, so on behalf of the whole church Lutherans should return repeatedly to Luther's theology for fresh insights. Similarly, the Augsburg Confession was clearly intended as a statement of faith offered to the whole church and not as a merely partisan declaration, so Lutheran attention to this confession can be fruitful for the entire church.

2. Another Lutheran *charism* is its serious reading of the human situation as thoroughly marked by the alienation of sin. This is not a popular message, for it contradicts many of our assumptions about the basic health and freedom of the individual. Within Christian circles as well, this understanding of the human condition is a minority perspective, yet it serves to call attention to elements of human experience that might otherwise be overlooked.

3. The central *charism* is the Lutheran message of justification by grace through faith. Among most Christian families, the primary emphasis falls on the transforming, sanctifying power of God's grace. This is true in Roman Catholicism, the largest Christian family. It is also true in the Orthodox churches, which constitute the second-largest group. Sanctification is also primary among most Protestants including Baptist, Methodist, Reformed, Evangelical, and Pentecostal. The Lutheran tradition is unique in placing the paramount accent on God's merciful acceptance of people. To be sure, all other Christian traditions acknowledge and proclaim God's acceptance, but in one way or another, it tends to be secondary. In the Lutheran heritage, acceptance is primary.

This message of justification by grace through faith is needed as much today as it was at the time of the Reformation. Granted, today there are few people plagued with a conscience that tells them to perform lots of religious rituals; that form of religiosity has died for most. What endures, though, is a profound need to be at peace with God, oneself, and others. The message of justification is easily watered down to merely forgiveness for specific acts we have done wrong. In fact, many Christians understand forgiveness mainly as an early stage in the Christian life, a stage one moves more or less beyond into the more significant stage of sanctification. What we discover, though, as our relationship with God continues, is that there are ever deeper levels of our life in need of acceptance. The message of God's unconditional acceptance is profoundly healing. God's unconditional acceptance is the heart of the Lutheran teaching of justification by grace through faith.

Of course, the good news of God's unconditional acceptance is not peculiar to the Lutheran tradition; it is part of the gospel that all Christian communities proclaim. When that whole gospel is proclaimed, people are confronted with all the gospel's saving power. Then they are most likely to have a balanced relationship with Jesus Christ that includes both unconditional acceptance and renewal. However, it frequently happens that portions of a Christian community get off track in their relationship with Christ, and their message gets out of balance. Those traditions that emphasize most the transformative, sanctifying power of God grace tend to get off balance by turning holiness from a work of grace into a human work. That's called "works righteousness." Since nearly all Christian traditions put the primary accent on renewal or sanctification, when they go wrong they share a tendency to slip into works righteousness. In this situation, it is extremely valuable to have the Lutheran community whose primary emphasis is on God's generous mercy that forgives freely.

Of course, Lutherans also are subject to works righteousness. Yet unlike most other Christian groups, when the Lutheran community gets off track, it often goes in the opposite direction as other Christian traditions. Forgiveness is taken for granted. Justification becomes a doctrine affirmed without being rooted in the experience of a living relationship with Jesus Christ. Then Lutherans do not experience either genuine acceptance or renewal. They coast along, going through the motions of religiosity, and believe they're doing just fine. What Lutherans need, then, is a reminder that what counts is genuine trust in Jesus Christ that brings both forgiveness and renewal. Lutheranism's own history is marked with such calls by Arndt, Spener, Kierkegaard, Bonhoeffer, and others. In fact, Dietrich Bonhoeffer's

Hitler era critique of "cheap grace" (forgiveness without transformation) and call for "costly grace" (forgiveness with transformation)
became so well known that his terms have become common usage.[8]
Often these efforts to get Lutherans back on track were nourished by
attention to other voices in the wider Christian tradition as well as
study of Scripture and Lutheran sources. In other words, Lutherans
have also benefited from the *charisms* of other traditions, even as
those other traditions have benefited from the Lutheran *charism* of
justification by grace through faith.

The fact that a community has been given a *charism* by God does
not guarantee that the *charism* will always be fully utilized. Indeed,
historical experience shows repeatedly that a *charism* needs to be
recovered again and again. The Roman Catholic order of Jesuits discovered this after the Second Vatican Council when they took a new
and deeper look at the Spiritual Exercises created by their founder,
Ignatius Loyola. The result has been a number of fresh applications
of that retreat format. Among Lutherans the three-hundred-year
anniversary of the Reformation in 1817 occasioned a new look at
Luther's teachings, and the early years of the twentieth century
brought the so-called Luther Renaissance that again revitalized
Lutheranism. Today I think the challenge for Lutherans is to explore
additional means by which the message of justification by faith may
connect with people's lives. For example, while the confession of sin
and announcement of absolution in the liturgy is valuable, something else is needed to actually reach the hearts and minds of many
with the gospel. For some people, a small group that delves into the
teaching may make it come alive. For others private confession or
one-on-one spiritual direction is a marvelous way to let the healing
of God's grace touch their lives. Of course, there is no technique by
which we can manage this work of the Holy Spirit, but fresh pathways
sometimes open new territory.

4. A great musical tradition is another Lutheran *charism*. Of
course, there are other Christian communities with outstanding
music as well, but the Lutheran heritage of fine art and congregational music is a gift that continues to make the word live in worship
and devotion.

5. An important Lutheran *charism* is its dialectical or paradoxical approach to social ethics. This dialectical approach that stresses the twofold rule of God has received much criticism since Hitler's rise to power in Germany. Nevertheless, its realistic stance is an extremely valuable contribution today when people so often have inflated expectations of a certain political, social, or intellectual movement. The paradoxical vision clearly distinguishes what such cultural movements can accomplish from what the gospel can accomplish. Even the evangelical historian of American religion, Mark Noll of Wheaton College, said this Lutheran perspective is needed as a balance in American political thought to the predominant approach that comes from the Reformed tradition.[9]

6. A valuable *charism* of Lutheran spirituality is an attitude that combines deep respect toward core Christian traditions with freedom to employ a variety of secondary traditions. This attitude is very well suited to our present cultural situation. On the one hand, Lutheran spirituality is solidly rooted in the core of the Christian tradition as expressed in Scripture and the classic creeds. As many Lutherans are fond of saying, this is a catholic as well as evangelical tradition. On the other hand, Lutheran spirituality has a freedom to employ a variety of personal and communal practices of worship and devotion. There is freedom to borrow from others, including those who are not Christian, as long as the practice is integrated with the core of salvation by grace through Jesus Christ. This stance gives stability and depth in practices centered in the gospel of Jesus Christ along with freedom to explore fresh ways to nurture faith.

In a time when many people are seeking spiritual resources for themselves and perhaps their family, the Lutheran family of spirituality represents a way of life full of grace. In chapters 2 through 8 of this book, we examined seven characteristics of Lutheran spirituality. (1) The conviction that humans are truly in bondage and need God to set us free. (2) Confidence that God's merciful grace undergirds all of life. (3) Primary reliance on the word of God to nourish faith. (4) Significant attention to sacraments and other physical symbols as means through which God's grace touches our lives. (5) Connection with Christian community, church, both for giving and receiving nurture in faith. (6) Commitment to core Christian traditions along with respectful freedom toward secondary traditions. (7) A dialectical or paradoxical approach to ethics that stresses God's twofold rule and God's call to serve others in everyday life.

This tradition certainly has weaknesses, but it also has considerable strengths and special gifts, or *charisms*. Healthy Lutheran spirituality is a way of life full of God's overflowing grace. Being grounded in that generous divine love makes it possible for us to move gracefully through the joys and sorrows of life.

For Reflection and Practice

1. Where are you now in your own spiritual life? Do you feel lost? At home? Headed in the right direction? Looking for help? Other? Give yourself time to ponder this issue, for it involves reflecting on the landscape of your life. You may find it helpful to close your eyes.

2. Continue reflection on your own spiritual landscape and perhaps of those closest to you. What strengths or *charisms* do you see? What areas need change or growth?

3. Is there balance in your life? That is, is there some degree of balance among work, play, worship/prayer, group time, private time? Take adequate time to reflect on this; don't rush. As you consider this matter, are you aware of any longing? What does this longing tell you?

4. If you have had experience with the Lutheran tradition, what do you personally regard as its greatest weakness? Its greatest strength?

If one or more of the above exercises are done in a group, first give ample time for individual reflection before group sharing begins.

NOTES

PREFACE

1. Bernard McGinn, "The Letter and the Spirit: Spirituality as an Academic Discipline," *The Cresset* 56, no. 7B (June 1993), 13–22.

2. The position paper, "Spirituality and Spiritual Formation," agrees when it says, "We have no Lutheran resources in spirituality which are not themselves already involved with wider Christian traditions of belief and practice." (Lutheran Theological Southern Seminary, 1998), 3.

1. CONTEXT PRESENT AND PAST

1. Augustine, *Confessions,* Basic Writings of Saint Augustine, vol. 1, ed. W.J. Oates (New York:: Random House, 1948), 3.

2. This is the result of the 1988 poll. Seventy-eight percent answered yes in 1957. In the more turbulent time of 1964, opinion fell, slightly, to 67 percent. George Gallup Jr. and Sarah Jones, *100 Questions and Answers: Religion in America* (Princeton: Princeton Religion Research Center, 1989), 76.

3. Wade Clark Roof and William McKinney, *American Mainline Religion: Its Changing Shape and Future* (New Brunswick: Rutgers University Press, 1987), 57.

4. Robert Wuthnow, *The Restructuring of American Religion: Society and Faith Since World War II* (Princeton: Princeton University Press, 1988), 88.

5. Gallup and Jones, *100 Questions and Answers,* 198.

6. Dean Hoge, Benton Johnson, and Donald Luidens, *Vanishing Boundaries: The Religion of Mainline Protestant Baby Boomers* (Louisville: Westminster/John Knox, 1994), 82.

7. I have adapted ideas from Meredith B. McGuire, "Mapping Contemporary American Spirituality: A Sociological Perspective," *Christian Spirituality Bulletin* 5 (Spring 1997): 3–6.

8. Robert Wuthnow, *After Heaven: Spirituality in America Since the 1950s* (Berkeley: University of California, 1998), 14–18; 168–98.

9. Thomas Moore, *Care of the Soul: A Guide for Cultivating Depth and Sacredness in Everyday Life* (New York: HarperPerennial, 1994), 260.

10. "Seeking Christian Interiority: An Interview with Louis Dupre," *The Christian Century* 114 (July 16–23, 1997): 655.

11. My definition of *spirituality* has some overlap and differences with that used in the position paper from Lutheran Theological Southern Seminary. The position paper uses a separate term, *spiritual life,* for faith itself, whereas my concept of spirituality includes faith. The position paper uses *spirituality* as "intentional practice of the Christian faith, both corporate and individual, insofar as it seeks to build up Christian identity and nurture 'life in the Spirit' in the multiple dimensions of personal existence." See "Spirituality and Spiritual Formation," 2. Their use of *spirituality* refers to what I call a path, except that in my usage the path not only nurtures a faith but includes expression of it. Since there is no universally accepted definition of *spirituality,* it is important to know how a particular person or document uses it.

12. In this discussion of the meaning of *spirituality,* I am distinguishing between an anthropological concept of spirituality as a human quest and a theological concept of spirituality as gift of God's Spirit. Both dimensions have their place.

13. For example, by Philipp Nicolai, *Lutheran Book of Worship (LBW)*, Hymns 31 and 76; in *Lutheran Worship (LW)*, Hymns 177 and 73. By Paul Gerhardt, *LBW*, Hymns 23 and 116; in *LW*, Hymns 19 and 113.

2. OUR HUMAN CONDITION

1. Since God is beyond gender and is spoken about in Scripture with predominantly male but also female metaphors, I will alternate use of both masculine and feminine pronouns for God.

2. Martin Luther, Small Catechism, in *The Book of Concord*, ed. Theodore G. Tappert (Philadelphia: Muhlenberg, 1959), 342. Also *Martin Luther's Basic Theological Writings,* ed. Timothy F. Lull (Minneapolis: Fortress Press, 1989), 476.

3. TRUST IN GOD'S MERCIFUL GRACE

1. "Lutherans Say . . . 5" (June 1991). Numbers for options added. Department for Research and Evaluation, Evangelical Lutheran Church in America.

2. A very clear example of Luther's teaching on these two forms of grace occurs in his treatise "Against Latomus," *Luther's Works,* 32:226–229. See also his "Two Kinds of Righteousness," *Luther's Works,* 31:297–300, and his "Lectures on Galatians—1535," *Luther's Works,* 26:229–230. My interpretation of

Luther on justification is supported by Paul Althaus, *The Theology of Martin Luther*, trans. Robert C. Schultz (Philadelphia: Fortress Press, 1966), 224–250, and the Finnish Luther scholar Simo Peura, "Christ as Favor and Gift: The Challenge of Luther's Understanding of Justification" (paper presented at conference in Northfield, Minn., June 1, 1996).

3. Formula of Concord, *Book of Concord*, 539–46. In this discussion, the Formula of Concord notes that sometimes the term *regeneration* included both aspects of grace.

4. Martin Luther, "The Freedom of a Christian," *Luther's Works*, 31:351–52; Timothy F. Lull, ed., *Martin Luther's Basic Theological Writings* (Minneapolis: Fortress Press, 1989), 603–4.

5. Ibid., *Luther's Works, 355*. Lull, *Luther's Basic Writings*, 607.

6. Two examples of this interpretation of justification are given by Richard J. Perry, and Simon S. Maimela in *Theology and the Black Experience: The Lutheran Heritage Interpreted by African and African-American Theologians* (Minneapolis: Augsburg, 1988), 16–19, 38–41.

7. See Mary Pellauer, "Conversation on Grace and Healing," *Lift Every Voice: Constructing Christian Theologies from the Underside*, rev. ed., ed. S. B. Thistlethwaite and M. P. Engel (Maryknoll: Orbis, 1998), 183–85.

8. James M. Kittelson, *Luther the Reformer* (Minneapolis: Augsburg, 1986), 40–41.

9. Lilly Gracia Christensen, "I Would Give Thanks," *Lutheran Woman Today* (May 1996): 48. "I Would Give Thanks" is copyright © Lilly Gracia Christensen and used by permission.

4. RELIANCE ON THE WORD OF GOD

1. Martin Luther, The Smalcald Articles, Part III, Article IV, *Book of Concord*, 310. Lull, *Luther's Basic Writings*, 527.

2. There is a difference in Old Testament books recognized as canonical by Protestant churches and the Roman Catholic Church. This divergence stems from the fact that Protestants generally recognize only those books in the Hebrew Bible, while Roman Catholics accept the larger number of books included in the ancient Greek translation of Hebrew writings called the Septuagint. This difference does not have much effect on doctrine.

3. "The Inspiration of Scripture," *A Report of the Commission on Theology and Church Relations*, The Lutheran Church—Missouri Synod (March 1975), 7–15.

4. Martin Luther, "Preface to the Epistles of St. John and St. Jude," *Luther's Works*, 35:396; also *Martin Luther: Selections from His Writings*, ed. John Dillenberger (Garden City: Anchor, 1961), 35–36.

5. Quoted by Regin Prenter in *More about Luther* (Decorah, Iowa: Luther College Press, 1958), Martin Luther Lectures, 2:73.

6. Martin Luther, "Sermon on the Sum of the Christian Life," *Luther's Works*, 51:262.

7. Martin Luther, "Concerning the Order of Public Worship," *Luther's Works*, 53:11

8. Martin Luther, "Ten Sermons on the Catechism," *Luther's Works*, 51:144.

9. Martin Luther, Large Catechism, *Book of Concord*, 379.

10. Martin Luther, "A Simple Way to Pray," *Luther's Works*, 43:193–211.

11. *For All the Saints: A Prayer Book for and by the Church*, 4 vols. (Delhi, N.Y.: American Lutheran Publicity Bureau, 1994–95).

12. Historically Lutherans have been more accustomed to group spiritual direction as that happened in Bible study groups, prayer groups, or pietist conventicles, yet one-to-one spiritual direction is also a valuable practice. One-to-one spiritual direction is also approved in the position paper of Lutheran Theological Southern Seminary, "Spirituality and Spiritual Formation," 5–6.

13. The Southern Seminary position paper strongly affirms the meditative and speaking *(oratio)* dimensions of prayer, but is silent on the contemplative dimension. Although Lutherans have questioned certain practices often associated with a contemplative way of life, it seems that we should approve contemplative prayer itself as another manifestation of God's grace and a profound way in which God communicates with us. Especially so when we claim, as does the position paper, to identify with the great ecumenical tradition. "Spirituality and Spiritual Formation," 3, 5.

14. Andrew Wilson-Dickson, *The Story of Christian Music* (Minneapolis: Fortress Press, 1996), 16–56.

15. A hymn may be broadly defined as a poem set to music in which the poem is not directly taken from Scripture, although it may be based upon Scripture.

16. Martin Luther, "Preface to George Rhan's Symphoniae iucundae," *Luther's Works*, 53:323.

17. Martin Luther, "Preface to the Wittenberg Hymnal," *Luther's Works*, 53:316.

18. Gracia Grindal, "To Translate Is to Betray: Trying to Hand the Lutheran Tradition On," *Dialog*, vol. 33 (Summer 1994): 184–85. Grindal distinguishes between the hymn tradition and the song tradition among Lutherans.

19. Gracia Grindal, "Dano-Norwegian Hymnody in America," *Lutheran Quarterly,* 6, 3 (Autumn 1992): 301–6. See also Gracia Grindal, "The Swedish Tradition in Hymnals and Songbooks," *Lutheran Quarterly,* 5, 4 (Winter 1991): 461–65.

20. Wilson-Dickson, *Story of Christian Music,* 191–206.

21. Grindal, "To Translate is to Betray," 190.

5. MEETING GOD IN PHYSICAL SYMBOLS

1. Luther says, "Yet, if I were to speak according to the usage of the Scriptures, I should have only one single sacrament, but with three sacramental signs. . . ." in "The Babylonian Captivity of the Church," *Luther's Works,* 36:18. Lull, *Luther's Basic Writings,* 274.

2. Martin Luther, Smalcald Articles, Part III, Article VII, *Book of Concord,* 312. Lull, *Luther's Basic Writings,* 529.

3. Philip Melanchthon, Apology of the Augsburg Confession, Article XIII, *Book of Concord,* 211–13. Also Article XI, 180, and Article XII, 187.

4. Augsburg Confession, Articles XI and XII; Apology of the Augsburg Confession, Articles XI, XII, XIII; Smalcald Articles, Part III, Articles VII and VIII; and both the Small Catechism and Large Catechism have sections that instruct and exhort regarding confession.

5. Martin Luther, Small Catechism, *Book of Concord,* 348. Lull, *Luther's Basic Writings,* 484.

6. A third metaphor for baptism in the New Testament is rebirth, but this meaning is grounded in Paul's earlier affirmation of baptism as dying and rising with Christ. cf. Arland J. Hultgren, "Baptism in the New Testament: Origins, Formulas, and Metaphors," *Word and World* 14,1 (Winter 1994): 10–11. The rebirth metaphor frequently occurs in the Lutheran confessions, e.g., Augsburg Confession, Article II, *Book of Concord,* 29.

7. Luther, Large Catechism, *Book of Concord,* 445.

8. The nearly universal practice of not rebaptizing is testimony to the permanence of God's promise in baptism. Those who practice only believer baptism will baptize someone who had undergone infant baptism, because they regard the previous rite as not a valid baptism. But if someone who has accepted believer baptism later becomes a Muslim and then returns to a believer baptism church, that person is ordinarily not rebaptized. The question is, When baptism is understood strictly as a person's outward testimony of faith, why not rebaptize? If a couple divorces and then decides to become husband and wife again, they must go through a second ceremony in which they make new vows. Similarly, a believer baptism understanding of baptism would seem to require rebaptism. So the ancient practice of not rebaptizing

speaks against understanding baptism as simply an outward testimony of a person's inner faith.

9. The Reformed/Presbyterian tradition has included two views of Christ's presence: the memorial view stemming from Ulrich Zwingli and the spiritual presence view held by John Calvin. Calvin's teaching is that while Christ's body is in heaven, believers are united with him through the Holy Spirit.

10. Luther, Small Catechism, *Book of Concord*, 352. Lull, *Luther's Basic Writings*, 489. Here Luther says whoever believes the words *for you* and *for the forgiveness of sins* "has what they say and declare: the forgiveness of sins." He ignores other meanings.

11. Luther, Large Catechism, *Book of Concord*, 457–61.

12. Luther, Smalcald Articles, Part III, Article VIII, *Book of Concord*, 312–13. Lull, *Luther's Basic Writings*, 529–32.

13. Luther, "A Brief Exhortation to Confession," Large Catechism, *Book of Concord*, 458.

14. The Southern Seminary position paper recognizes that spiritual discipline will vary with individuals, yet says, "But every Christian's personal discipline should be founded on the remembrance of Baptism, centered in eucharistic worship, and reflect the normative pattern of Christian formation" (the last meaning engagement with God's word and prayer). "Spirituality and Spiritual Formation," 5. This is very theologically correct. Focus on Word and Sacrament as means of grace is vital, and a practice such as remembrance of baptism should be recommended. However, I think we should be less prescriptive. It would be less than helpful for pastors and spiritual directors to see their first task as trying to get people to conform to this threefold pattern. A spiritual director should begin by listening to how God is already touching a person's life. Then it is important to encourage that person to engage Scripture and other forms of God's word, and experience the sacraments. Yet it might well be that, say, remembrance of baptism never becomes a very significant part of a mature Christian's spiritual life, although the underlying reality of dying and rising with Christ would be. The Holy Spirit may have ways of conforming a person to Jesus Christ that don't neatly employ all three of these components. Nonetheless, I agree that regular involvement with the gospel is essential for Christians.

6. CHRISTIAN SPIRITUALITY AND THE CHURCH

1. John Wilson and Darren E. Sherkat, "Returning to the Fold," *Journal for the Scientific Study of Religion* 33 (June 1994): 148–61.

2. Wade Clark Roof, *A Generation of Seekers: The Spiritual Journeys of the Baby Boom Generation* (San Francisco: HarperSanFrancisco, 1993), 154–61.

3. George Gallup Jr., conversation with author, Spirituality and Healing conference, Houston, Texas, March 1998.

4. Ayn Rand, *The Virtue of Selfishness* (New York: New American Library, 1964), vii–xi.

5. The other stages in order are: primal faith, intuitive-projective faith, and mythic-literal faith, and the seventh stage is universalizing faith. James W. Fowler, *Becoming Adult, Becoming Christian: Adult Development and Christian Faith* (San Francisco: Harper & Row, 1984), 52–71. Earlier Fowler distinguished six stages of faith, but called primal faith a pre-stage. James W. Fowler, *Stages of Faith: The Psychology of Human Development and the Quest for Meaning* (San Francisco: Harper & Row, 1981), 119–21.

6. Fowler, *Stages of Faith*, 181–82.

7. Ibid., 180–81.

8. Fowler, *Becoming Adult, Becoming Christian*, 66.

9. See Martin Luther's explanation to the third article of the creed, Large Catechism, *Book of Concord*, 416–17. Also Melanchthon's formulation of the church as "the assembly of all believers among whom the Gospel is preached in its purity and the holy sacraments are administered according to the Gospel." Article VII of the Augsburg Confessions, *Book of Concord*, 32.

10. Martin Luther, "Freedom of a Christian," *Luther's Works*, 31:355. Lull, *Luther's Basic Writings*, 607.

11. I borrow and adapt this terminology of Big Story from Alex Garcia-Rivera via Philip Hefner, "The Demographics of Possibility: People's Church," *Currents in Theology and Mission*, vol. 25 (August 1998): 295–302.

12. "Talking to God," *Newsweek*, 6 January 1992, 39.

13. Dean R. Hoge, Benton Johnson, and Donald A. Luidens, *Vanishing Boundaries: The Religion of Mainline Protestant Baby Boomers* (Louisville: Westminster/John Knox, 1994), 204–5. This is a study of baby boomers who had been confirmed in the Presbyterian church as youth, so the sample is not a true cross section of all baby boomers.

14. "A Lutheran Stance toward Ecumenism," 9–11. This is a 1974 report of The Lutheran Church—Missouri Synod (LCMS) Commission on Theology and Church Relations. While this statement has not been formally approved by the LCMS national convention, it is the most reliable expression of the synod's overall ecumenical stance.

15. *Book of Concord*, 32.

16. "Ecumenism: The Vision of the Evangelical Lutheran Church in America," 4–5. This is a policy statement adopted by the ELCA Churchwide Assembly in 1991.

7. CHURCH TRADITIONS

1. *Vanishing Boundaries: The Religion of Mainline Protestant Baby Boomers* (Louisville: Westminster/John Knox, 1994), 115.

2. *Social* pluralism refers to the undeniable fact that there are many different groups and perspectives in the world. *Theological* pluralism goes further by giving a relativistic interpretation to this social reality. Relativism means not only the fact that perspectives and beliefs vary with different cultural contexts but that no perspective is more true than any other.

3. An influential scholarly version of theological pluralism is articulated by the philosopher of religion John Hick who views the morality of compassionate love as the core. See John Hick, *An Interpretation of Religion: Human Responses to the Transcendent* (New Haven: Yale University Press, 1989), 240.

4. Hoge et al., *Vanishing Boundaries*, 116.

5. There are other forms of inclusivism as well, such as Islamic inclusivism or Hindu inclusivism. In fact, appearances to the contrary, I think the various versions of relativistic pluralism really amount to a moralistic inclusivism, for they claim their outlook is more true than others.

6. Both Christian exclusivism and inclusivism are consistent with trinitarian teaching.

7. After Vatican Council II (1962–65), the Roman Catholic Church also adopted these three changes.

8. Article XV, Apology of the Augsburg Confession, *Book of Concord*, 222. Article XV of the Augsburg Confession on ecclesiastical rites also says, "Our churches teach that those rites should be observed which can be observed without sin and which contribute to peace and good order in the church. Such are certain holy days, festivals, and the like.

Nevertheless, men are admonished not to burden their consciences with such things, as if observances of this kind were necessary for salvation. They are also admonished that human traditions which are instituted to propitiate God, merit grace, and make satisfaction for sins are opposed to the Gospel and the teaching about faith." *Book of Concord*, 36–37.

9. Since the Anglican, or Episcopal, church also retained the Western rite, their eucharistic services are very close to Lutheran and Roman Catholic.

10. For a thoughtful defense of alternative worship, see David S. Luecke, *Evangelical Style and Lutheran Substance: Facing America's Mission Challenge* (St. Louis: Concordia, 1988).

11. Frank C. Senn, "'Worship Alive': An Analysis and Critique of 'Alternative Worship Services,'" *Worship*, vol. 69, no. 3 (May 1995): 194–224. See also Frank C. Senn, *Christian Liturgy: Catholic and Evangelical* (Minneapolis: Fortress Press, 1997), 687–92.

12. James F. White, *Protestant Worship: Traditions in Transition* (Louisville: Westminster/John Knox, 1989), 22–23.

13. Ibid., 211.

8. SERVICE IN DAILY LIFE

1. Another major aspect of God's creativity is to provide new possibilities. One mechanism for doing this is randomness or chance in matter and evolution. Although randomness is often viewed as opposed to purpose, it need not be. After all, we human beings devise card games and other games that involve both rules (order, law) and chance. We create extra difficulty for ourselves when we expect every dimension of every event to be purposive. Would it not be better to view the world as a combination of order and randomness?

2. Contemporary Lutheran ethicist Robert Benne characterizes our social roles as being sanctioned, dynamic (changing), and ambiguous. See Robert Benne, *Ordinary Saints: An Introduction to the Christian Life* (Minneapolis: Fortress Press, 1988), 70.

3. Herbert Benson, M.D., *Timeless Healing: The Power and Biology of Belief* (New York: Scribner, 1996), 195–99.

4. "The spiritual and the earthly governments constitute two kingdoms, but both of these are God's. They are not in opposition to one another, but, side by side, both contend against the devil, one guided by the gospel, and the other by the law." Gustaf Wingren, *Luther on Vocation*, trans. Carl C. Rasmussen (Philadelphia: Muhlenberg, 1957), 85.

5. In the discussion of vocation that follows, I have borrowed freely from Benne, *Ordinary Saints*, 129–73.

6. A clear, brief discussion of three types of self-realization ethics (the most popular type above is called romantic self-discovery) is given in *The Westminster Dictionary of Christian Ethics*, s.v. "Self-realization."

7. I understand *work* as any activity that produces services or products of value. Work is not synonymous with occupation or job, and not all work is paid. Yet in common usage, *work* is often more narrowly understood as paid labor.

8. H. Richard Niebuhr, *Christ and Culture* (New York: Harper, 1951).

9. Larry L. Rasmussen, "A Community of the Cross," *Dialog*, vol. 30 (Spring 1991): 150–62. This Lutheran ethicist proposes a theology of the cross as the organizing principle for ethics. Robert Benne, *The Paradoxical Vision: A Public Theology for the Twenty-First Century* (Minneapolis: Fortress Press, 1995), 26–43. As non-Lutheran exponents of the paradoxical vision, Benne claims the great American ethicist Reinhold Niebuhr and contemporary political philosopher Glenn Tinder; the latter, although not a member of the Lutheran Church, explicitly identifies himself with the

Lutheran outlook. See Glenn Tinder, *The Political Meaning of Christianity: An Interpretation* (Baton Rouge: Louisiana State University, 1989), 2–3.

10. Benne, *Paradoxical Vision*, 138.

11. Advocacy is different from lobbying. Whereas lobbyists work for their organizations' self-interest, advocates speak for the interests of others, especially the vulnerable.

9. TAKING STOCK

1. Ninian Smart, *Dimensions of the Sacred: An Anatomy of the World's Beliefs* (Berkeley: University of California, 1996), 8–14. Also Ninian Smart, *The World's Religions* (Englewood Cliffs: Prentice Hall, 1989), 12–21.

2. *The Westminster Dictionary of Christian Ethics*, rev. ed.,1986, has no entry on Baptist ethics, although it has entries on Calvinist, Lutheran, Methodist (Wesleyan), and Roman Catholic ethics.

3. *The Westminster Dictionary of Christian Spirituality*, s.v. "Baptist Spirituality."

4. When asked in a survey How essential are certain elements in your vision of the Catholic faith? the number one answer of Roman Catholics age 20–39 was belief in God's presence in the sacraments. Also very high was devotion to Mary. William Dinges, Dean Hoge, Mary Johnson, and Juan Gonzales Jr., "A Faith Loosely Held: The Institutional Allegiance of Young Catholics," *Commonweal* (17 July 1998): 13–18.

5. *The Westminster Dictionary of Christian Ethics* , rev. ed. (1986), s.v. "Modern Roman Catholic Moral Theology."

6. The Vatican's response to the *Joint Declaration on the Doctrine of Justification* crafted by Lutheran and Roman Catholic theologians listed eight reservations, the first of which was to the Lutheran teaching of the Christian as at the same time righteous and a sinner. *Forum Letter* 27, 8 (August 1998): 1–2.

7. "Women in the Church: Scriptural Principles and Ecclesial Practice," a report of the Commission on Theology and Church Relations of The Lutheran Church—Missouri Synod, 18–38.

8. Dietrich Bonhoeffer, *The Cost of Discipleship*, rev. ed. (New York: Macmillan, 1959), 35–47.

9. Noll also identifies the Lutheran confessions and Luther's theology as treasures that Lutherans have to offer Americans. Mark A. Noll, "The Lutheran Difference," *First Things*, vol. 20 (February 1992): 38–40.